WRAP Yourself In The Word

WRAP
Yourself
In The
Word

A Simple Practice in Scripture
that Leads to Hope and Healing

Joni Rosebrock

WRAP Yourself in the Word

Copyright© 2024 by Joni Rosebrock

Library of Congress Cataloging-in-Publication Data

LCCN: 2024903637 ISBN: 978-1-961732-18-6 (ebook) |

ISBN: 978-1-961732-19-3 (paperback) | ISBN: 978-1-961732-20-9 (hardcover)

Published in association with Called Creatives Publishing, www.calledcreativespublishing.com

Cover design: *Called Creatives Publishing*

Interior design: Joni Rosebrock

2024 - First Edition

Table of Contents

Chapter One

Begin to WRAP Yourself in the Word

But do not be afraid. The simple fact that you are more aware of your wounds shows that you have sufficient strength to face them. Your heart is greater than your wounds.

Henri Nouwen

I drove by a house near the busy highway on my way to work. I watched for the lonely swan, usually swimming in the pond before the house. I saw the realtor's sign and the swan walking in the grass near the busy highway. It wasn't swimming in the pond before the house. He was all alone in the grass. Why was he standing so near the road, and why was he alone? I went online to learn more about this mysterious swan when I arrived at work. It was before Google became widely used, so I probably went to "ask Jeeves" for answers. (Side note: Ask Jeeves is now ask.com.) The internet confirmed that swans live in pairs and often die of broken hearts if left alone. And this felt significant because this was the first day back to work after the sudden death of my stepdad, Bob. I worried about how I would handle my grief and help my mom, a young widow, navigate this loss. The lonely swan was a reminder of our loss.

The next day, the swan was by the road again - his wings spread wide and flopping up and down like he was about to take flight. Just then, he wrapped one wing under the other. It was strange behavior, reminding me of my brother and his silly six-year-old friends when they discovered they could make farting sounds by putting one hand under the opposite armpit and pumping their arm up and down.

The swan's shenanigans made me smile, and I thought, "Thanks, Dad, I miss you too." Every day for more than two months, as I drove to work, I saw that swan near the road walking in the grass. It truly comforted me to think that maybe God placed the swan there as encouragement from my dad every morning. God used that swan to remind me of my dad's love and let me know I was not alone.

During that time of my life, I experienced profound spiritual growth. I used my daily commute time to talk with God, listen to His Word, and listen to Him. Going past this property 20 years later, even though it is abandoned, I still look for a swan. You never know.

The time in my car to and from work was a rich blessing. I prayed and God listened. God spoke and I listened. He allowed me to dream and think about things I wanted to create and do. The ideas and dreams I logged in the several years driving back and forth were seeds He planted and are now becoming a reality in my life. A lot of life happened between that time and now. Our kids grew up and graduated from high school. I left the career I loved, started a new business, and then closed that business several years later.

I got lost. I moved far away from the dreams God had planted in my heart. Regret and shame covered the seeds; I thought they had died in the cold darkness.

I found myself going through the motions of life, doing what I thought everyone expected of me. I learned how to keep from disappointing others by hiding things and stuffing my needs. I soon discovered I had no joy and was no joy to be around.

Most days, I wanted to go to bed or not get out of bed. Sleeping was my only rest. My heart had drifted far from God, although most people didn't know it. I still attended church every Sunday, led my youth group on Wednesday nights, and taught Bible study on Tuesday mornings. I did a great job of hiding the deep sadness and torment. I functioned as well as I could, owning two businesses, helping my husband with farming, and being a mom to two of our three children still at home, one in college and one in high school.

One day, my husband came home with news I was unprepared to hear - like someone ripping off a sticky adhesive bandage stuck to a festering wound. My heart raced, my body shook, and I could not settle down. I wanted to throw things and scream at anyone or anything. That day, the intense emotion drove me to tears and uncontrollable anger. No, not anger – rage. All the pent-up frustration, disappointment, and bitterness that boiled inside the volcano of my heart exploded out all over my life, and I was not okay.

The trigger was simple: Someone did not do what I expected them to do professionally, and I could not change the situation. It was a permanent decision that I did not like. These actions utterly devastated me. He did nothing wrong, but I disagreed with his choices, which also impacted my family's financial opportunities. His choice affected how I pictured my life playing out over the next few years. I spent the weekend angry, crying, and in bed. Just like volcano eruptions are often unpredictable, the eruption of all the ugly stuff in my heart unexpectedly exploded because of this seemingly simple action.

I remember the gut-wrenching sobbing. The injustice of the situation infuriated me. It made no sense to me. I was mad that I was caught off guard and disappointed I had let something push me so far off center. I was an emotional mess. Whatever degree is past hot mess, that was me.

> Thank God He had protected my mind and heart to have the presence of mind to seek help.

And this moment exposed the wound, the ugly infection in my heart. The only coherent thought I remember was, "I need help." Thank God He had protected my mind and heart to have the presence of mind to seek help. I called the doctor, and the nurse gave me the number of a Christian Counselor who could see me the following week.

The visit to the counselor began a two-year journey of walking through deep caverns, exposing the emotional pain of silent bubbling lava in my heart. While uncovering

4

and refining was difficult, God never left my side. Through every breakthrough and heartache, I began to see His faithfulness and gentleness as God molded my desires, thoughts, and behaviors to reflect His design for my life.

The messy middle was one of the most complex parts of my healing journey. I was not walking in complete obedience to God's Word and was deeply aware of my sins, mess, and shortcomings. I know I am somewhat vague in not telling you exactly what was going on, but the details are not essential, and I frankly am not ready to share them. There was no infidelity or juicy episode like that other than I thought everyone knew my shortcomings and was the talk of gossip. That is a bit of paranoia. That's what shame does, no matter what the cause.

That's why I am writing this book—to share with you that messy middle, to walk alongside you as you journey from pain and loss to hope and joy.

Trusting God with your story is a brave thing to do because you also have to trust yourself. When you are the one who got you into the mess, it is hard to work through trusting again. Here's what I know on this side of hope and healing: crying out to God in honest desperation is the first step in the trust process. Being honest with yourself and allowing God to shape how you see yourself and others is life-changing.

Later, I will share more about the healing journey and how God's faithfulness sustained me when I couldn't look forward. He began to teach and lead me through a process I can only see now as I reflect. I trusted Him, but I had no idea where He was taking me. His gentle presence guided me as He cleansed me and provided hope when I could not begin to see a way out. First of all, He reminded me daily to seek His Word.

My journey through deep emotional healing, family reconciliation, and spiritual strengthening began as I wrote God's word daily. This was the beginning of God drawing me closer to Himself using His Word to lay the foundation for the next step. Much of what God taught me was so intimate that I didn't share it with anyone, including my husband or closest friends. Only now, as I look back, can I see what God gifted me: WRAP Yourself in the Word.

I remember sitting in my office one day, reflecting on my healing, and wondering what God had in store for me next. I was praising Him for His faithfulness and seeking guidance on a few decisions I needed to make. I was looking over a few notes on my journey as I was trying to map out what had happened in my life over the past five years. I noticed the key movements of God's guidance and my responses, and there it was. I started by writing the Word and then reading more of His Word. I was curious. I noticed how I slowly transitioned to asking more questions about how what I was reading was relevant to my life. I was reading a book about praying

> I remember thanking God for being so faithful and good to me. I heard Him say to my spirit, "You have wrapped yourself in my Word."

6

for God's Word at that time, and I noticed the words write, read, ask or apply, and pray. I remember thanking God for being so faithful and good to me. I heard Him say to my spirit, "You have wrapped yourself in my Word." This brings me to tears just thinking about it.

Could it be that even after all these years, God was leading me back to His plan for my life and awakening the seeds He planted during those years of driving an hour to and from work every day? Yes, it is! You are reading evidence of what the Bible says in Romans 11: God's gifts and call can never be withdrawn.

WRAP is an acronym for Write, Read, Apply, and Pray. I will share more details on each part of the process in the following chapters. Of course, you don't have to do everything in this order or even as I explain. The beauty of each discipline is that you honor God in doing them, and growth will happen because of our obedience to being in His Divine Word.

I spent many months on the first step. I wrote Scripture for many days. I started in a journal and filled every page with one verse at a time. As I wrote God's Word faithfully, He expanded my curiosity, and I desired more. So, I began to read the verses in context before and after the verse I wrote in my journal. Soon, God led me to pray over the verses and seek His Word as it applied to me.

I also love that the word WRAP creates a picture in our minds. Maybe you think of a special Christmas gift wrapped in beautiful paper and adorned with the most spectacular handmade bow. Or perhaps you see yourself in a cozy chair wrapped in a soft, fuzzy throw, sitting with

7

your favorite mug filled with a hot, yummy beverage. Whatever comes to your mind as you encounter God's Word, I pray it will boldly lead you to a sweet surrendering of your time, heart, and life as you WRAP Yourself in the Word.

I also pray you do not view this book as a quick fix because it isn't. My intent in sharing what I learned is not to say, "If I can do it, you can too." Because I didn't do it, God did. Yes, I participated, but He is responsible for the outcome. My most profound prayer is for God's Word to open your eyes and heart to see His Faithfulness and Grace through His Word. It is only by the Word of God that we can honestly know ourselves and intimately know our Savior. And knowing Jesus is the best gift we could ever receive.

> It is only by the Word of God that we can honestly know ourselves and intimately know our Savior.

Write

Write the verse.

The process begins by writing out a specific verse or passage of Scripture. Here are a few suggestions to get you started.

- Use a Scripture writing plan. The 90-Day Scripture Writing Plan I used is accessible via the QR code in the resource section of this book.

- Start in any chapter of any book of the Bible and write a verse at a time.

- Write verses your pastor uses in his weekly sermons.

- Write verses from a book you are reading. I found this a great way to enrich my reading experience.

- Google a topic. "What does the Bible say about ...." And write the verses related to your chosen topic.

- Look up a verse online and write it out in different translations.

Get a journal or tablet and get started. You can also use 3x5 note cards and keep them in your purse or computer bag. Write every day.

Read

Read the verse.

After you write the verse, read what you wrote. First, read it to yourself as you have written it. Second, read it out loud. You may have a negative flashback of elementary school reading out loud. I promise this is not like that. The experience of hearing God's Word read by your voice is exciting and powerful as you build this practice. A third way to add to this experience is to read the verse to someone out loud. Pretend you're reading it to a group of students or friends. You may feel self-conscious, but it's ok. The more you practice this, the easier it becomes.

Apply/Ask
Apply the verse.

The easiest way to implement this step is to ask God to show you how to apply this verse to your life. What does God want me to think, feel, or do in response to this verse? Whatever questions you ask and seek to apply, be sure to listen and reflect on what you hear God whispering to you in response. (You may be wondering, "Does God really whisper or talk to you?" and the short answer is yes, through the Holy Spirit, I believe He does.)

You can also ask yourself: Is there a promise, instruction, or command in this verse? Where do I need God's help applying them in my life? What is the most important thing God wants me to see or know in this verse?

Pray
Pray the verse.

Prayer seems to be a spiritual practice that many people need help implementing consistently. We know we need to pray, but it is sometimes one of those things we make more complicated than it is. Making it a part of the WRAP Yourself in the Word allows you to focus your prayer on the Scripture you wrote. You pray God's Word back to Him. You tell God what His Word says and ask Him to make it true in your life. We will practice this together throughout the book.

WRAP Yourself in the Word

Use Proverbs 3:5 ESV to WRAP Yourself in the Word.

Trust in the LORD with all your heart,
and do not lean on your own understanding.

Write
Write the verse.

Read
Read the verse.

Apply

Apply the verse.

What are the instructions in this verse?

Pray

Pray the verse.

Father, Your Word says we are to trust you with all our hearts. I don't know how to do that. Please help me understand and begin to trust you. Show me when I am leaning on my understanding, knowing I can trust you. Amen.

Honestly, it's that simple. God loves to hear our prayers and know we are reading His Word.

Start in small ways, and do not expect yourself to have it all figured out. God will honor your obedience to make time to be in His Word. He will delight in your willingness to pray and listen for His response. You are prioritizing your relationship with our Creator, which will be rewarded.

A personal note about the power of the Word of God:

How do you get to know a person you just met? How did you get to know your spouse, best friends, or the people you work with?

You spent time with them. You asked them questions and shared your stories. Maybe you discovered a common interest, and you talked for hours. I bet you had long, beautiful conversations and laughed and cried together. Your relationship with God and His Word is the same. You commit the time and emotional energy and get to know God through His Word.

At the end of each chapter, I suggest Scripture for your practice WRAP, along with other resources and sometimes a growth challenge. You'll see how it all works as we go along.

Thank you for picking up this gift, and I pray as Paul did in the letter he wrote to the people of Ephesus.

Ephesians 3:14-21 ESV

Father: I bow my knees before the Father, from whom every family in heaven and on earth is named, that according to the riches of his glory, he may grant you to be strengthened with power through his Spirit in your inner being, so that Christ may dwell in your hearts through faith—that you, being rooted and grounded in love, may have the strength to comprehend with all the saints what is the breadth and length and height and depth, and to know the love of Christ that surpasses knowledge, that you may be filled with all the fullness of God. Now to him who can do far more abundantly than all that we ask or think, according to the power at work within us, to him be glory in the church and Christ Jesus throughout all generations, forever and ever. Amen.

Chapter Two

Write the Word

First, I do not sit down at my desk to put into verse something that is already clear in my mind. If it were clear in my mind, I should have no incentive or need to write about it. We do not write in order to be understood; we write in order to understand.

C. S. Lewis

Do you have a committee inside your head? It seems to chatter relentlessly with opinions about every matter in your life. I do, too.

I am not talking about multiple personalities. I don't become different people. I am fully myself, but the inner voices seem familiar, usually condemning, and very rude. I used to joke about "my committee," thinking everyone had this experience. Most of the time, it was just my voice expressing different emotions. Often they were uninvited and loud. I tamed them by saying out loud that I was the chairwoman of this committee and did not call a meeting. It was an easy way to laugh about the disturbing noise in my heart and mind.

I had mastered managing this inner group of voices until that day when rage came oozing out of my soul. I couldn't stop the overflow of intrusive emotions. I knew it had become a serious problem when I didn't give a crap about how I expressed them or to whom. I was done holding in all the frustration, so I didn't seem ungrateful. I was done over-censoring my bluntness so I didn't alienate others. I was done stuffing the bitterness so those closest to me couldn't see and feel my deep hurt and sadness.

Here are some thoughts I often filtered from "my committee."

"Why are you so surprised by this?"

"You knew that it would never work out."

"Be grateful you have a house to live in."

"Go to bed. It will get better, or maybe you won't wake up."

"Maybe you should do what you tell others to do and pray or read your Bible."

"You better get your crap together; people depend on you. You have to fix this."

"Shame on you to expect something different. Your mistakes are the reason you are in this situation."

"Your husband is going to find out how you screwed up."

"You got yourself into this. Now get yourself out of it."

"I need a bottle of wine."

"I need to be alone."

'I was unsure what I expected the doctor to do. They were unlikely to see me this late Friday afternoon and were not in the office over the weekend. I just knew I needed help. More importantly, I wanted help.

For nearly 20 years, I managed it all with medication and lived a high-functioning life. I was on medication for depression, anxiety, and migraines. Maybe the doctor had something I hadn't considered to help me fix this.

I tried to explain what was going on without going into much detail about the trigger circumstances. Instead, I focused on what I had done that wasn't working and why I needed to see the doctor. The nurse asked me a few questions that I thought were unusual. But looking back, she was trying to assess if I was in danger of harming myself or anyone else. "You need to talk to someone," she said. I thought, "OK, that is why I am calling." I expected to be transferred to schedule an appointment, but instead, she gave me the number of a Christian counselor. "Tell them we referred you and ask to be seen soon."

I got through the weekend. The anger, despair, bitterness, and rage were still intense. I couldn't fix it, so I called the number of the Christian counselor the doctor provided. The counselor was able to fit me in that week.

First, we met weekly, then every other week, eventually monthly, and then we met only when I needed it. I met with my counselor for nearly two years. I had no clue what to expect. I took comfort in his being called a Christian counselor. His calm, caring demeanor was reassuring.

He compiled a road map of my family relationships during the first two or three visits. We discussed how these people communicated and related to me and each other as passive, aggressive, passive-aggressive, or assertive. My first homework assignment was a worksheet to help me discern the lies I believed versus the truth. This exercise helped me examine my self-talk. I thought, "Does he know what he is asking me to do? Does he really want me to expose the committee?" But, because he based this exercise on the truth of God's Word, I knew this would be a different counseling experience.

> Determining lie versus truth involved intentionally noticing the influences on my thoughts, feelings, and behaviors.

He labeled the top of the paper "Self-Talk" and drew a line down the middle. On one side of the page, he wrote "old messages – lies" and "new messages – truth " on the other. Under lies, he wrote "what if" thinking; under truth, he wrote "even if" thinking. Determining lie versus truth involved intentionally noticing the influences on my thoughts, feelings, and behaviors.

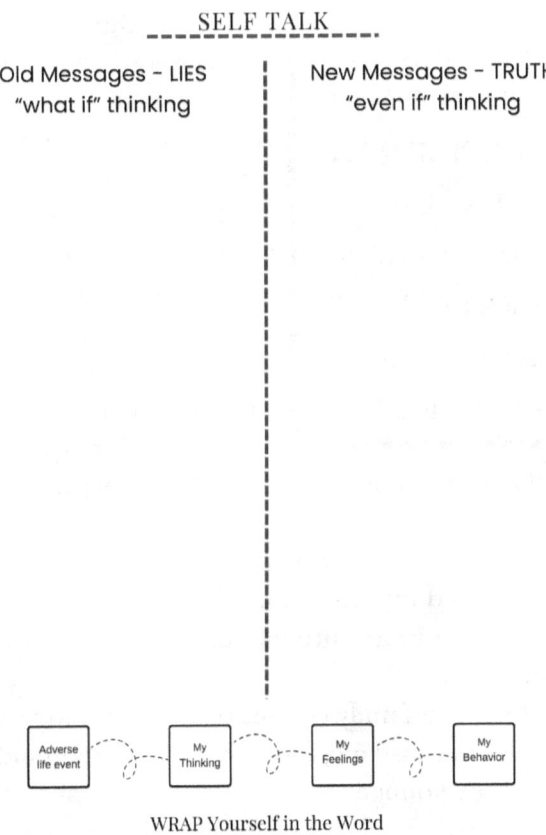

SELF TALK

Old Messages - LIES
"what if" thinking

New Messages - TRUTH
"even if" thinking

Adverse life event → My Thinking → My Feelings → My Behavior

WRAP Yourself in the Word
JoniRosebrock.com

Here's the flow he wrote out for me that day.

An adverse life event influences my thinking, which causes a feeling resulting in my behavior. This happens so quickly in our brain that it often seems automatic, making it difficult to distinguish what happens first. This process

> As I began to write out Scripture, the counselor gave me to refute the lie, the power of God's Word began working in my heart.

of getting it into my heart and mind through continued awareness of what was going on in my thoughts, feelings, and behavior was exhausting yet transformational.

Discerning the lies I believed was revealing and frightening, but looking at them through a lens of Scripture was comforting. As I began to write out Scripture, the counselor gave me to refute the lie, the power of God's Word began working in my heart.

I want you to know a little about who I was before the deep-rooted bitterness and dark depression seized my heart. I'll share more throughout the book, but here is a quick snapshot.

I belong to a family of amazing women. My mom was sixteen when she had me, and we lived with my grandparents and her three younger sisters. I was a cherished little girl who was surrounded by unconditional love. I was voted "Most Spirited" in my senior class, probably because I was a cheerleader all four years of high school and one year in college. I enjoyed people and being a part of lots of different friend groups. I loved school, learning, teachers, friends, and just being me. I got engaged my senior year and married my high school sweetheart. I was the girl who dreamed of being in love, being married, and having a family. I loved making memories and celebrating with my family. I looked at life through the proverbial rose-colored glasses. I wasn't naïve; I preferred seeing the good in people and life. I still do.

There were many adverse events, including the deaths of five grandparents, my parents' divorce, the deaths of three close classmates and friends, and, as a married adult, the heartbreak of losing a parent and more beloved grandparents. My life wasn't always sunshine and roses, but my extroverted personality was cheerful, confident, and creative.

How I Began Writing Scripture

I have loved writing my entire life. As a young girl, I wrote poems, stories, and skits. I didn't write in a diary, but I had a collection of great sayings and quotes I wrote in a notebook. I have always loved the physical act of picking up a great writing instrument and writing. I prefer a No 2 Ticonderoga pencil or a 7mm blue ink pen.

So, it was natural for me to begin writing when life got difficult. I started writing one verse at a time, beginning with the verses from counseling. Then, I came across a monthly Scripture writing plan on Pinterest and printed it off. Every day, I wrote one verse.

> Every day, I wrote one verse. I opened my journal, wrote the verse, and closed it.

I opened my journal, wrote the verse, and closed it. That was it. I did that for three or four months. Sometimes, my counselor would share more verses related to the counseling topic and homework that week, and I also wrote them in my journal.

One of the first changes I noticed was that the noise and frequency of "the committee" had faded. I no longer noticed such loud, intrusive thoughts and negative berating. Writing Scripture replaced lies with truth in my heart—God's Truth.

I want to share those first few verses to show you what God was saying. It will give you an idea of what the Word of God can do. I hope you see how this small act of obedience in writing a single verse of Scripture can change your heart. Remember, this is not a quick fix. God may not work in your life just like He did in mine. You may be dealing with different life circumstances, but I know you will notice God working in your heart if you write His Word consistently.

Philippians 4:8 NIV

"Finally, brothers and sisters, whatever is true, whatever is noble, whatever is right, whatever is pure, whatever is lovely, whatever is admirable—if anything is excellent or praiseworthy—think about such things."

This is a great verse to begin with because it speaks directly to our thoughts. I held all the negative thoughts and the chatter from my committee next to this way of thinking. I honestly remember thinking to myself, "I have a choice of what I can think about. I don't

> I have a choice of what I can think about. I don't have to let my mind boss me around.

have to let my mind boss me around." This verse gives me ammunition against the committee and reminds me that I also do not have to believe other people's opinions of me. My mom used to tell me growing up that other people's opinions of me are none of my business. She was right. She's going to be so happy to see that in writing. Every mom hopes her kids finally admit she is right.

2 Corinthians 10:5b NIV

"We take captive every thought
to make it obedient to Christ."

God's Word empowers us with the truth. We don't have to believe the lies that we think. We believe what we repeatedly tell ourselves, even if it is a lie. The first action in the verse is to take captive every thought. Like you capture a thief who has stolen property. Next, we are told to make it obedient to Christ. What does that mean exactly? I like to ask two questions, "Is this what Jesus thinks of me? Or would Jesus be pleased with this way of thinking?"

Romans 12:1-2 NIV

"Therefore, I urge you, brothers and sisters, in view of God's mercy, to offer your bodies as a living sacrifice, holy and pleasing to God—this is your true and proper worship. Do not conform to the pattern of this world but be transformed by the renewing of your mind. Then you will be able to test and approve what God's will is—his good, pleasing and perfect will."

I could write three chapters on these two verses, and later, we will discuss them, but I struggled to understand the point the counselor had for reading them, especially what God needed to teach me. What I did was what I am teaching you to do. I wrote the verse several times and asked God to show me what He wanted me to learn.

Benefits of Writing Scripture

One of the things that most surprised me when I started writing was how often I remembered the verse. Starting with a monthly plan of verses that share a common theme is helpful to retaining what you write. However, I also strongly believe that the physical act of handwriting is critical to engaging Scripture. Strong evidence suggests improved learning when students handwrite notes versus typing on a keyboard.

> One of the things that most surprised me when I started writing was how often I remembered the verse.

Research by Pam Mueller and Daniel Oppenheimer revealed that students who write their notes on paper learn more. The researchers had students take notes in a classroom setting and then tested their memory of the facts, understanding of the material, and ability to integrate and draw conclusions from the information. Half of the students took notes with a laptop, and the other half wrote the notes by hand. The researchers concluded that the brain processes taking notes by hand differently than taking notes on a laptop, and these different processes have consequences for learning.[1]

1 Mueller, P., & Oppenheimer, D. M. (2018). Corrigendum: The pen is mightier than the keyboard: Advantages of longhand over laptop note taking. *Psychological Science*, 29(9), 1565–1568. https://doi.org/10.1177/0956797618781773

Other handwriting benefits include:

- enhances learning, creativity, and problem-solving
- improves our cognitive performance
- allows us to experience relaxation
- process emotions and untangle thoughts
- helps us organize our thoughts as we evaluate our emotional conflicts - For example, my counselor asked me to keep a journal to track when I experienced the most anxiety.

Best of all, Scripture writing can deepen our faith by enhancing our ability to hide God's Word in our hearts through memorization and comprehension. (Psalm 119:11)

> Best of all, Scripture writing can deepen our faith by enhancing our ability to hide God's Word in our hearts through memorization and comprehension.

It helps us slow down and consider what the Word says. We draw on multiple areas of the brain to collaborate when writing and spend time thinking or meditating on the Word. (Psalm 1:2, Joshua 1:8)

Likewise, the physical activity of writing helps us retain and remember what we write. (Exodus 17:14, Jeremiah 30:2)

I will admit that I struggled a few times when life was busy. Honestly, my depression would often win the short-term battle and distract me. It wasn't easy to focus some days when I let the internal committee discourage me. But, when I discovered that I hadn't written for a few days, I caught up with the days I missed and started again.

This simple practice doesn't take much time, but obedience to God's Word is the most essential benefit. Begin today and write His Word every day. It's OK if you are not ready to complete the entire WRAP method daily. Start by writing one verse.

WRAP Yourself in the Word

Expand the verse from the last chapter and write out
Proverbs 3:5-6 ESV.

Trust in the LORD *with all your heart, and do not lean
on your own understanding. In all your ways submit to
him, and he will make your paths straight.*

Write
Write the verse.

Read

Read the verse.

1. Read it to yourself.

2. Read it out loud to yourself.

3. Read it to someone else.

Apply

Apply the verse.

In addition to God's instructions in this verse, can you note a promise or a benefit of obedience?

Pray

Pray the verse.

Father, Your Word says we are to trust You with all our hearts. I don't know how to do that. Please help me understand and begin to trust you. Show me when I am leaning on my understanding. Help me remember the benefits of your Word. I trust you to make my paths straight and show me which way to go as I seek your way instead of doing it my way. AMEN

Growth Challenge

Write the three verses I started with and shared above.

Chapter Three

Read the Word

*The word of God hidden in the heart
is a stubborn voice to suppress.*

Billy Graham

"I just want my wife back!" This had become my husband's desperate plea. He usually expressed it angrily as he tried to reach and relate to me. He wanted the wife he married and raised children with— the wife before bitterness, self-hatred, and depression consumed me and smothered our joy. My usual response was to look away from his disappointment-filled eyes and do something else. I didn't fight back, understand, or try to fix it. I had gone past the desire to understand what was wrong with me and fix it. I was tired of not being enough, not doing the right thing, and not acting like I used to. I was not me, and I had no idea who that person was, even if I wanted to fix it. I didn't know his wife.

This time, I yelled back. "Fine, tell me who she is, and I will be her." That was my answer. I could end all the darkness and unhappiness if he told me who she was. I could be her if I knew who she was and what he wanted. We could all be happy. That was my answer to fixing this situation. I honestly thought I could just be her if he could tell me who he thought his wife was. The problem with being who he needed me to be was that it wasn't truly who I was.

> I didn't understand that life would shake up my cheerful, confident, and creative self.

I was a joyful person. I saw the best in people. I often gave more than I received. I was ok with that. When I became more focused on pleasing other people, I lost myself. When I was more focused on the fear of disappointing others, I lost my identity as a child of God. I didn't understand that life would shake up my cheerful, confident, and creative self. I didn't know how to rewrite the story from the drama I created and the ongoing tragedy in my heart and mind. What had I done? Who was the woman my husband needed?

In his book, *When People are Big and God is Small*, Ed Welch addresses why we fear people.

"We fear people because they can expose and humiliate us, ridicule and reject us, and attack, threaten, or oppress us. These three reasons have one thing in common: they see people as "bigger" (that is, more powerful and significant) than God, and, out of the fear that creates in us, we give other people the power to tell us what to feel, think, and do."[2]

I love Ed Welch's books, but this one messed with me. I found myself in this book. It made sense to me. Just a few chapters into the book, as he elaborates on the fear of rejection, Welch says that our problem is not that we care about rejection. Rather, we hope the other person will return the favor and fill us with esteem, love, admiration, acceptance, and respect. When pleasing the people in our lives grows to oversized proportions, they become idols, and our idols control us. For the Christian, an idol is anything that takes the place of God as the most important priority in your life. (Exodus 20:3)

This helped me to see that my husband was an idol for me.

> For the Christian, an idol is anything that takes the place of God as the most important priority in your life.

Similarly, *In the Ways of God*, Richard Blackaby says idols are humanity's misguided attempt to downsize God to a level they can understand and control.[3] That pretty much paints the picture of what was brewing in my heart. As long as I could control everything, I could fix it.

2 Welch, E. T. (2023). *When People Are Big, and God Is Small: Overcoming Peer Pressure, Codependency, and the Fear of Man.* P & R Publishing.
3 Blackaby, R. (2023). *The Ways of God: How God Reveals Himself Before a Watching World.* B & H Publishing.

God Began to Move

I loved almost every day of high school and college. I loved my teachers, classes, and classmates. I truly enjoyed every experience. But this love of learning became my crutch, or an idol, in my heart. I was convinced I could escape the sadness if I gathered enough knowledge and understanding. I should be smart enough to figure a way out. I read every popular self-help book about the mind, thoughts, and habits. I read and trusted many famous Christian authors and considered their wisdom more valuable than God's Word. I thought they were people who had figured it out. Just one more book would help me fix this life of chaos I created. I spent money and time building a library of knowledge but not gaining wisdom. Acquiring knowledge and books became an idol for me.

My Tuesday morning Bible study leader challenged us to read the entire Bible from May to September. Who doesn't love a good challenge? I jumped in like I did so often. If everyone else was doing it, I surely could. It was hard to read without taking the time to study specific passages. The leader's goal for us was to read all the way through for an overall perspective of God's Word. I had become accustomed to studying chapters and books in depth, but I had never read the Bible from beginning to end. Something started happening in my heart when I read through the Bible. I found a context for the many verses I had written. God's story was being written in my heart.

This reading challenge revealed to me how knowledge and other books had become my focus instead of God's Word. Through the challenge, His Word became relevant to the most minor pieces of my life. I began to reflect and see how God had always been a part of

> I began to reflect and see how God had always been a part of my story.

my story. God was always there, gently leading me with His truth and faithfulness. I was the one who drifted, who became self-dependent. I was busy trying to control and fix my story while God was there all along, waiting for me to see that He was the writer of my story. He has already written the story.

What I also saw from reading the Bible cover to cover was a big story of flawed people and an even more important story of redemption, reconciliation, and forgiveness. I saw God's grace.

God gently called me to trust Him more profoundly by inviting me to read His Word and desire more. The popular wisdom of man, or even credible Godly authors who wrote with knowledge, could not fill me with what I needed. I learned that even those good works were not God's best for me. He desired me to know Him and trust Him, and the best way to know God is to spend time with Him reading His Word.

I found a God who knew me and wanted more for me than I could ever imagine. As I surrendered every day, every moment, every lie, every thought of shame, and every negative emotion, He revealed more of His goodness to me. He began to replace what was broken and hurting with hope and joy. This was the Holy Spirit at work in me.

The Benefits of Reading God's Word

I also want this same testimony about reading God's Word for you, Dear One.

Start where I did. As you make time to write a passage each day, start reading the few verses above or below the passage. Reading the subtitles in your Bible is also helpful. A word of caution: If something seems odd or you don't understand what you are reading, I encourage you to do two things.

> Stop and pray about what you are reading. Ask the Holy Spirit to help you.

1. Stop and pray about what you are reading. Ask the Holy Spirit to help you.

2. Consider reading more than the adjacent verses. Taking the Bible out of context is harmful. Many well-meaning Christians use verses as weapons to judge. This is dangerous. Understanding the intent, content, and context of God's Word is important.

The goal is to begin reading.

Bible-reading strategies are more accessible now than ever. There are wonderful audio Bibles available on your phone or computer. Hearing someone read the words to you as you follow is a powerful learning tool. Hearing and seeing the phrase enforces the activity in different brain regions, enhancing comprehension. I'll list some of my favorites in the resources section at the end of the book.

My favorite way to read the Bible is by reading the original scrolls. No, I'm just kidding! I love to hold the physical book in my hands, turn pages, read the footnotes and cross-references, and look up verses. I am so grateful that I memorized the order of the books of both the Old and New Testaments when I was a child in Vacation Bible School.

Get started!

1. Read the verse(s) silently to yourself.

2. Read it out loud to yourself. It may feel uncomfortable but trust me: You can do it! Reading the Bible aloud was commonplace throughout history. It was the only way most people had access to the Bible. (Nehemiah 9:3, 8:8, 1 Timothy 4:13)

3. Read it to someone else. Pretend you read it to a group of students or a good friend.

Reading as part of the WRAP Yourself in the Word method is designed to help you encounter Scripture personally and intimately. It builds on the discipline of writing and will help you remember the Scripture. When I struggle to comprehend what I am reading, I read it out loud. Hearing and seeing the words helps me with understanding and focus.

God's Word comes to life with your voice.

WRAP Yourself in the Word
Revelation 1:3 NIV

Blessed is the one who reads aloud the words of this prophecy, and blessed are those who hear it and take to heart what is written in it because the time is near.

Write

Write the verse.

Read

Read the verse.

1. Read it to yourself.
2. Read it out loud to yourself.
3. Read it to someone else.

Apply
Apply the verse.

Is there a promise, instruction, or command in this passage? Based on the verse, what does God want me to do, think, or feel?

Pray
Pray the verse.

Father, I trust you and look forward to the blessings of reading your Word. Help me take it to heart and seriously consider your Word for my life. AMEN

Growth Challenge

Locate the table of contents of your Bible. Work at memorizing the order of books of the New Testament. It is a convenient skill.

If you would like to begin reading the Bible in addition to reading as part of the WRAP method, I have a few suggestions:

To know Jesus more deeply, start with the Gospel of John. The purpose of John's Gospel is found in John 20:30-31.

> *So then, many other signs Jesus also performed in the presence of the disciples, which are not written in this book; but these have been written so that you may believe that Jesus is the Christ, the Son of God; and that by believing you may have life in His name.*

John walks us through the relationship with Jesus and His disciples and others. It contains many words spoken by Jesus. This Gospel is written so that we will believe that Jesus is the Son of God.

To learn more about who you are in Christ, start in the book of Ephesians. This book fills our hearts with the truth of who we are as we sit with Christ, how to walk in His ways, and finally, how to stand against what opposes us in spiritual battles. We will spend time in Ephesians in several chapters.

You can also choose to jump around in the book of Psalms. It is the songbook of the Bible, filled with praise and rejoicing, lamenting, and crying out to God. You will find comfort and encouragement as you relate to the writers. Most people think King David wrote the Psalms, but he only penned half of them. Other writers include Asaph, the sons of Korah, Moses, Solomon, and others.

Of course, the challenge of reading the entire Bible is always an option. There are many good plans to help you do it. Check out the resources for my favorites.

Chapter Four

Apply the Word

*The essence of surrender is getting out of
God's way so that He can do in us what
He also wants to do through us.*

A.W. Tozer

Most of the time, struggling through depression was like drowning in water twelve feet from shore, and the rope God threw out to rescue me was only ten feet long. I couldn't reach Him. I couldn't swim on my own to get closer. The more I struggled to reach the rope, the wearier I grew. Something had to give. I could go on striving to fix the circumstances, or I could surrender and trust God.

It was hard learning that I wasn't the fixer. My husband wasn't the fixer. Work, denial, alcohol, spending, gaining more knowledge, trying new things, none of it was the fixer. What I mean by "fixer" is that no one or nothing could take away the discouragement and restore joy to my life - not my husband demanding his wife back or the monthly crate of wine on auto-delivery.

> God was the only fixer, and I had to trust Him to do the fixing.

God was the only fixer, and I had to trust Him to do the fixing. Yes, something had to give, and it was me. I had to accept responsibility for my thoughts, emotions, and how I responded to the lies of my situation. I had to surrender the striving, denial, and the fact that I was not well. I had to trust that God could handle all of me and my mess. His Word tells us in Matthew that we can come to Him, and His burden is light.

Matthew 11:28-30

Then Jesus said, "Come to me, all of you who are weary and carry heavy burdens, and I will give you rest. Take my yoke upon you. Let me teach you, because I am humble and gentle at heart, and you will find rest for your souls. For my yoke is easy to bear, and the burden I give you is light."

Jesus calls all of us to come to Him, but in this passage, He is talking to those burdened by their spiritual woes because they, like me, were trying to save themselves. Rest - that is what I needed. Jesus invites us to take His yoke, which He is comparing to the Pharisees or the law. Picture a large beam that is heavy and burdensome on the shoulders of two oxens. The goal of the yoke is to keep the animals together and to go in the same direction, pulling the load and completing the farmer's work.

Jesus is saying that he carries this yoke for us. The total weight of the law and the burden of our striving, sin, and disobedience is placed on Jesus's shoulders. He makes the yoke easy because of who He is and His sacrifice on the cross for us. We can learn from Jesus's humble and gentle heart without judgment and condemnation of the law. He will teach us. He wants us to walk with Him and connect ourselves to Him, and He will carry the heavy weight of our burdens. That's why He says the burden is light and easy.

So here is what I take away from this: If what I am carrying feels too heavy and I am struggling, there is something I have not surrendered. I need to seek Jesus. Please understand me. We will suffer and go through hard things. That is not what this passage is saying or what I am advocating. We will suffer, and we will have difficulty in this life. But we can do it alone in our weakness, striving, or yoked to Jesus.

> If what I am carrying feels too heavy and I am struggling, there is something I have not surrendered. I need to seek Jesus.

One of the Bible's analogies (and stories that use ordinary everyday things to inspire and move us toward God) is the picture of a yoke. As a farmer's wife, this

47

connected something I knew about to a truth Jesus was teaching. Asking questions and applying God's Word to our lives can be that simple. With this idea and hope that Jesus would carry my burdens, I began to cry out to Him.

Trees are another analogy frequently found in Scripture. God used my love for trees to make another heart connection to His Word. The tree depicted in Psalm 1:3 was the opposite of what I was feeling and experiencing, and I desperately wanted to be like that tree. I cried out for months and months. I prayed this prayer daily.

"Lord, I want to be like that tree. Plant me firmly by your living waters so my roots grow deep into your refreshing streams of truth. I will not thirst in times of drought because your living water is running through me. Father, create fruit in me to grow in the seasons you had established for me before I was born. Father, please don't let me wither. I do not want to be this way ever again. I want to be alive and flourish in what You have called me to do and created me to be. I never want to wither. Father, please let me prosper in all I do. I want my life to bring you Glory."

I was tired of being me. I was ready to surrender my way and live according to His. And thankfully, God lovingly taught me about His ways. It's a continual process, but I love it.

He gifted me with the WRAP Yourself in the Word practice, and before that, He led me through Psalm 1 with lovingkindness. This week, I was reading *The Ways of God* by Richard Blackaby, and I was reminded that God's ways are sequential. I found this to be true when He guided me

48

through Psalm 1, but Blackaby brings a little more clarity for me, and I thought you also needed to know about it.

"God always acts in a planned, effective, methodical manner. This is one of the ways in which God is highly predictable. His ways are sequential, not random. God takes no shortcuts, is not impulsive, and never panics. Understanding the sequential way God acts will greatly enhance our ability to recognize and anticipate his work in and around our life."

Blackaby explains that God is masterful in preparation as He works through and in people, often starting small and working through seasons in our lives.

"God has built systems, principles, and seasons into the fabric of creation. He has determined that we reap what we have sown. He desires to produce a bountiful harvest in and through us. He is willing to take all the time necessary to help us grow and mature for this to happen. For us to embrace God's will for our life, we must follow God's prescribed order for living."

Why didn't God tell me this? Isn't it like us to want it all wrapped up in a neat little package or paragraph? Unlike God, we are impatient, impulsive, and panicky if we lack understanding. The journey I describe below is exactly what Blackaby highlights in his book. I didn't know what God was doing. Let's face it, that's a good thing because I probably would have rushed ahead and started striving on my own all over again.

See if you can pick out the process God leads me through. Here's what Psalm 1:3 says about the tree.

Psalm 1:3 ESV

He is like a tree planted by streams of water that yields its fruit in its season, and its leaf does not wither. In all that he does, he prospers.

> God began teaching me that my deep emptiness, where I longed for something more, was my desire to know more about Him.

God began teaching me that my deep emptiness, where I longed for something more, was my desire to know more about Him. I thought I had lost God, but I hadn't. I moved away from Him, filled my life with other voices, and could not sense His presence. God never moves away from us.

Occasionally, I would have a flicker of hope in my soul. It came as a familiar voice but not condemning like the other voices in "my committee." It was encouraging, peaceful, and inviting. At first, I ignored the voice like I tried to do with the others. But this voice got louder and stayed loving, warm, and gentle. I began to listen. This voice pursued me through the discipline of writing, reading, and every word of Scripture. It answered my cry to know Jesus and be like the tree in Psalm 1.

I prayed repeatedly, asking God how I could be like this tree.

His Answer

Psalm 1:2 ESV

But they delight in the law of the LORD,
meditating on it day and night.

Honestly, this took me weeks to unpack. I started studying that single verse word by word. This was a revealing study for me. It helped me dig into God's Word. It helped me understand that the familiar voice I was hearing was the voice of Truth, but the only way to hear that voice was to delight in and meditate on God's Word. I'll teach you how through WRAP Yourself in the Word. It is a way to think about and apply God's truths.

God was slowly replacing all the negative and condemning voices with His voice of love and truth! Praise God from whom all blessings flow! Please understand that this was not an overnight miracle. Please do not compare what you may or may not experience to what you perceived happened in my life. Our journeys are different, but our God is the same, and He is able.

> Our journeys are different, but our God is the same, and He is able.

Psalm 1:1 ESV

Blessed is the man who walks not in the counsel of the wicked, nor stands in the way of sinners, nor sits in the seat of scoffers.

This verse says we are blessed if we don't walk, sit, and stand with these negative people. Was I doing what God says I should not? Was I missing His blessing? I could be blessed. I felt like I had some explaining to do. I didn't think about who I walked with or the sinners I stood with, let alone the scoffers in my life. What are scoffers anyway? Dear One, I am here to tell you that this pruning process was uncomfortable, especially when I discovered I was a wicked, scoffing sinner.

My point in sharing this is to show you the process.

1. I cried out – make me like the tree in verse three.

2. God told me how in verse two – delight and meditate on His Word.

3. Evaluate how I was living – verse one.

Benefits of Applying God's Word

Asking questions to apply God's Word in our lives requires us to approach His Word with

1. A surrendered heart to listen.

2. Open ears to hear the truth.

3. Willingness to change our behavior.

When we ask questions of God, He will faithfully answer them. I began asking questions of God like:

- How do I meditate and delight in your Word?

- What does the walk in the way of the wicked look like?

- Where do I stand with sinners?

- Who are the scoffers, and how do I avoid sitting with them?

The Ask/Apply step in the WRAP Yourself in the Word is a mini version of an inductive Bible study where we seek to Observe, Interpret, and Apply God's Word. If you want to learn more about this type of study, I include a bonus chapter on my website where I DIG (Discover, Investigate, and Grow) into Psalm 1:1-3. It is my simplified version of an inductive study. You can find access to this and the other resources mentioned in this book by using the QR code in the back of the book or going directly to my website, jonirosebrock.com.

Write

Write the verse.

Since we are going to spend time in Psalm 1:1-3 in later chapters, I have a different passage for you to WRAP:

WRAP Yourself in the Word

"Come to me, all of you who are weary and carry heavy burdens, and I will give you rest. Take my yoke upon you. Let me teach you, because I am humble and gentle at heart, and you will find rest for your souls. For my yoke is easy to bear, and the burden I give you is light." Matthew 11:28-30 NLT

Read
Read the verse.

1. Read it to yourself.

2. Read it out loud to yourself.

3. Read it to someone else.

Apply
Apply the verse.

Look at the cause and effect in this passage. If I do _____, God will do _____. or If God does _____, then I can be _____.

- If I come to God weary of my burdens, He will give me rest.

- If I take His yoke, He will teach me. Why? What qualities does Jesus have that allow Him to teach us?

- Because of who Jesus is, I can have rest.

Pray

Pray the verse.

Father, I want to rest and surrender my heavy burdens. I am tired of being weary. Teach me how to take up the yoke of Jesus. Help me to make a daily choice to walk with Jesus and learn from Him. Jesus, thank you for your humble and gentle heart. Thank you for the provision to rest as I trust in You. Thank you for Jesus's sacrifice to carry my selfishness and burdens to the cross. AMEN

Growth Challenge:

Read Psalm 119.

Make two columns on your paper. In the first Column, list what you learn about God's Word, His attributes, or His power as you read Psalm 119. Then, in the second column, list how you think or feel or what you are to do in response to His Word. Use the QR code in the back of the book to access a chart on the website that breaks this Psalm into sections for you to study.

Chapter Five

Pray the Word

Prayer turns theology into experience.
Timothy Keller

Have you ever been in a situation where your dependence on God was all you had to depend on? This was us when my sister-in-law was diagnosed with stage 4 breast cancer, and we received a call from her that she was in the hospital. From the day of that call, we started making plans to be more active in her care and hopefully convince her to come live with us two hours away in Ohio. Several times throughout the year, my husband asked me, "Will we be the same after this?"

We prayed many times over the year, "Father, give us the wisdom to know what to say. Help us love her well." We knew it was the right thing to do, but we had no idea how it would all work out. We knew the end was in her death, but before that, we just wanted her to be in our home and know she was loved.

My sister-in-law lived alone most of her life in Michigan. She never married and was a University of Michigan fan.

My husband is a graduate of The Ohio State University. If you're not familiar with college football, these two universities probably have the biggest rivalry in college football. We had some good fun in that situation. She got to see U of M beat the Buckeyes in the big November game. She didn't even rub it in, but she was so happy.

I started writing this book shortly after she moved in with us. The three of us had deep theological and sociological conversations. And sometimes, when her brother wasn't around, we had some good girl talk. My sister-in-law was kind, witty, and intelligent. I appreciated her perspective so much. She came to know and love Jesus while she lived with us, and we rejoice, knowing we will see her again.

During this hard season of life, the WRAP Yourself in the Word practice again allowed me to connect to God more deeply. I used it to study, meditate, and pray God's Word back to Him. Sometimes, the only words I had to pray were God's Words. I would look up Scripture on suffering, trials, death, heaven, and more. I went through the same steps.

> During this hard season of life, the WRAP Yourself in the Word practice again allowed me to connect to God more deeply.

I share this little bit of her story with you only because we made it through that year due to our dependence on God and our constant prayers. I also want you to know that WRAP isn't just applicable to depression and anxiety. You can use it daily to study, pray, and meditate on God's Word, no matter your struggle or suffering.

What is Prayer?

Jesus modeled a prayerful life and instructed us to pray, so we know it is important. We know that it is an essential tool in our relationship with God, and I believe we intellectually understand that prayer is powerful. Moving the idea of believing something to experiencing transformation is more difficult yet essential in our Christian walk.

Prayer is sometimes seen as an elusive concept that only the most scholarly or mature Christians master. If that were true, I would not be writing this book and sharing the benefits I have experienced through prayer. Prayer is one of those things we make too complicated. I believe that is because we listen to the wrong voices: ourselves and Satan.

One of my all-time favorite preachers is the late Tim Keller. In his book, *Prayer: Experiencing Awe and Intimacy with God*, he defines prayer as a personal, communicative response to the knowledge of God. Keller suggests that if prayer is our response to the knowledge of God, then our prayers are impacted by the amount and accuracy of our knowledge of God. That makes sense to me. Conversations with the people we know change as our relationships grow deeper, and that's how it works with God. We must spend time with His Word to grow in knowledge. WRAP

> Conversations with the people we know change as our relationships grow deeper, and that's how it works with God.

Yourself in the Word gives you the process of building your knowledge of God.

Keller explains: "Prayer, then, is a response to the knowledge of God, but it works itself out at two levels. At one level, prayer is a human instinct to seek help based on a very general and unfocused sense of God. It is an effort to communicate, but it cannot be a real conversation because the knowledge of God is too vague."[4]

It was my instinct to cry out, and I had a vague sense of God when I desperately needed Him. Through the counsel of God's Word, writing, reading, and asking questions about applying it to my life, my knowledge of God grew.

---

4 Keller, T. A. (1963). *Prayer: Experiencing Awe and Intimacy with God.*

How Do We Pray?

There are thousands of books and resources on how to pray. However, I believe a simple model to follow is the Lord's Prayer, which is found in Matthew 6. Jesus begins by telling the disciples what not to do.

- Don't be a hypocrite by standing on street corners praying so the attention rewards you.

- Don't babble on as other religions do.

- Jesus gives instructions on how to pray better.

- Get away by yourself behind a closed door for privacy.

- Trust that the Father sees everything and knows what you need.

Any prayer can be modeled after the Lord's Prayer.

1. Worship: Praise, honor, and thanksgiving - Matthew 6:9 "Our Father in heaven, hallowed be your name."

2. Surrender: Lay it down – Matthew 6:10: "Your kingdom come, your will be done, on earth as it is in heaven."

3. Petition: Asking for our needs and for others' needs – Matthew 6:11: "Give us today our daily bread.

4. Confession and Forgiveness: Clears the way for God's blessings - Matthew 6:12 "And forgive our debts, as we also forgive our debtors.

5. Guidance and Protection: Trust Him to lead us and deliver – Matthew 6:13: "And lead us not into temptation but deliver us from the evil one.

6. Worship: End in praise – Matthew 13b found in the King James Version. "For thine is the kingdom, and the power and the glory forever, AMEN."

For example, a prayer for your morning may go like this: Father, you are the creator of everything. We praise you for your wisdom and might. As I begin my day, I surrender my day to you. Move in me to say and do things that are pleasing to you. Father, I am sorry for the angry words I said last night. Please forgive me. Help me also forgive the things that hurt my feelings that my husband said. He is also a child of God. Help me see him as you see him. Father, I need wisdom for the decisions I have to make today. I want them to be pleasing to you. Guard my heart as I engage in conversations with others and protect me from any distractions that Satan will throw in my way. You are always with me. Thank you for your kindness and love. AMEN

> Guard my heart as I engage in conversations with others and protect me from any distractions that Satan will throw in my way.

Satan will throw obstacles in our way to keep us from the important work of prayer. He will try to convince you that:

- You don't know how to pray.

- You don't know what to pray.

- You're not good at it.

- God didn't say to pray that way.

- God won't hear your prayers.

- God already knows, so why pray?

Doubt the doubts that Satan will throw at you. When you feel inadequate, tell God you are struggling. Romans 8:26 says, "And the Holy Spirit helps us in our weakness. For example, we don't know what God wants us to pray for. But the Holy Spirit prays for us with groanings that cannot be expressed in words."

> Doubt the doubts that Satan will throw at you.

My healing journey started when I was desperate and cried out to God. Is crying out the same as prayer? I think so. It was for me.

Psalm 18:6

But in my distress I cried out to the LORD; yes, I prayed to my God for help. He heard me from his sanctuary; my cry to him reached his ears.

Psalm 34:17-18

The LORD hears his people when they call to him for help. He rescues them from all their troubles. The LORD is close to the brokenhearted; he rescues those whose spirits are crushed.

I trusted God to cry out, and He led me to His Word. Once I rested in His yoke and trusted Him to carry my burdens, I could delight in His Word. He then guided me to examine my life and discover the things that needed to go.

Psalm 139:23-24

Search me, O God, and know my heart; test me and know my anxious thoughts. Point out anything in me that offends you and lead me along the path of everlasting life.

Proverbs 3:11-12

My child, don't reject the LORD's discipline, and don't be upset when he corrects you. For the LORD corrects those he loves, just as a father corrects a child in whom he delights.

Hebrews 12:10-11

God's discipline is always good for us, so that we might share in his holiness. No discipline is enjoyable while it is happening—it's painful! But afterward there will be a peaceful harvest of right living for those who are trained in this way.

Benefits of Praying God's Word

When you WRAP Yourself in the Word, you allow God to transform your heart. Through writing, reading, applying, and praying God's Word, the Holy Spirit works in you to sanctify and make you more like Jesus.

After God showed me the next step in Psalm 1:1, I began praying for God to show me where I was missing His blessings or where I was missing the mark in my life. I asked God in prayer to show me:

- Where am I walking in the advice or counsel of the wicked and ungodly people?

- Where am I taking a stand with wrongdoers or sinners?

- Where am I sitting or dwelling with scoffers who mock You and show contempt with insulting words and actions?

> Praying God's Word is just saying His Words back to Him.

Praying God's Word is just saying His Words back to Him. Look at the power we have in God's Word. Here are a few powerful passages of Scripture. I encourage you to commit them to memory and pray to God daily.

Hebrews 4:12 ESV

For the word of God is living and active, sharper than any two-edged sword, piercing to the division of soul and of spirit, of joints and marrow, and discerning the thoughts and intentions of the heart.

Father, your Word is living and active. Make it new in my heart and show me your truth. Let your Word cut through the dead areas of my heart and my thoughts, exposing where I need help. Forgive me for the darkness and doubt and renew my thoughts and actions so they will please you. Amen.

You may also need prayer to oppose false teachings. This verse can be prayed in response to others as well.

Father, help me discern the thoughts and intentions of the people I encounter through your living and active words. Let your Word guide me, direct me through the lies, and show me what is true and trustworthy. Amen.

John 17:17 ESV

Sanctify them in the truth; your word is truth.

Father, continue to make me holy, set apart, and sanctified as I read and study your truth. Amen.

2 Timothy 3:16-17 ESV

*All Scripture is breathed out by God and profitable
for teaching, for reproof, for correction, and for
training in righteousness, that the man of God may be
complete, equipped for every good work.*

Father, your Word is breathed out by you for our benefit. It is how you teach, correct, and train us to be holy like you are holy. Equip me through Your Word and in all that You have planned for me. Thank you for your faithfulness and for loving me. Amen.

Write

Write the verse.

We looked at a lot of Scripture in this chapter. For practice, use :

WRAP Yourself in the Word

Psalm 34:17-18 - The LORD hears his people when they call to him for help. He rescues them from all their troubles. The LORD is close to the brokenhearted; he rescues those whose spirits are crushed.

Read

Read the verse.

1. Read it to yourself.

2. Read it out loud to yourself.

3. Read it to someone else.

Apply

Apply the verse.

What instructions, commands, and promises do you see in this passage? What does God want me to think, feel, or do in response to what this passage teaches?

Pray

Pray the verse.

Father, You hear me when I cry out or quietly pray to you. You are faithful in responding and rescuing me from trouble. Remind me that you are always near me, especially when I need you and am brokenhearted. AMEN

Growth Challenge

Review the chapter and WRAP each verse in your journal.
Take as many days as you need.

Chapter Six

A Full-Time Faith

The Christian does not think God will
love us because we are good, but that
God will make us good because He loves us.

C.S. Lewis

When the kids were still home, I drove them around in a bright yellow Volkswagen GTI with a turbo six-speed. Yes, it went fast! I loved driving that car, and they loved riding in it. Her name was Sunshine. Most people called it a clown car because all five of us would pile in it and climb out of it like clowns in a circus car. I would tell them, "Get in, buckle up, and hold on!"

There were several times God probably could have told me, "Get in, buckle up, and hold on!" As I began to hear God's voice of truth more clearly over other voices, I could also see Him weaving this thread of faithfulness in my heart and mind, creating a story of freedom, identity, and fruitfulness. Prayer and Scripture were only two of the tools He used to speak to me over the years.

I knew Jesus loved me growing up. He was the constant thread through my childhood. At eight years old, at Vacation Bible School, I understood I needed Jesus for my salvation. I began my faith journey that day, although I know my grandma's prayers continued to impact my life.

My grandma's love, actions, and prayers are why I know Jesus, and I often went to church on Sunday with her and my grandpa. I would rather spend every day with them, which I am sure made Mom a bit frustrated, but I always wanted to go to Grandma's house. My grandma's legacy of faith had the most significant impact on my childhood, and I look forward to the day she and I will spend time with Jesus again.

I am fortunate to have the legacy of a faithful family who made church attendance necessary throughout my growing-up years. When my mom remarried, she and my stepdad insisted we go to church as a family, which impacted my teenage years. When my husband and I decided to get married, I joined his church so our children would be raised in a family with the same religious traditions. We attended a church his grandparents helped build, as he also had a family legacy of faith.

When our children were ages 18, 15, and 10, we left the church they had grown up in, searching for a greater understanding of Jesus. That was a life-changing decision for all of us. At the time, we felt it was necessary because of our unique circumstances. It allowed our family to experience a deeper faith than a family legacy and religious traditions. Please understand what I am saying. I am not telling you that religious traditions are wrong. Your experience may differ, and I hope you find great comfort in your church. We did not.

What is Your Faith Legacy?

Could we meet for tea or coffee and share our faith stories? I imagine us sitting on the Pour it Out Porch. The porch on our newly renovated farmhouse is inviting and comfy. The perfect place to pour out our burdens and prayers to the Lord and each other. It is a warm early summer day in Ohio, with a pleasant breeze on the farm. Luckily, the neighbor hasn't recently hauled natural fertilizer (chicken poop) on the field across the road. I'm just adding some reality lest you think the farm life is too romantic. I could ask you, "I've shared some of my journey. What is your faith story?"

Do you know where you would start sharing your faith story? Have you put your faith in Jesus? I have assumed you have already put your trust in Jesus Christ and have experience in God's Word. If you haven't and sense the need to accept Jesus as your Savior and Lord, I am honored to lead you through the following experience. Pastor Tim Keller is noted for saying that the Gospel changes everything. I believe it does!

Ask God to speak to you as you read the following Scripture. You may have heard this referred to as the "Roman Road" because it takes you through passages in Romans to help you see the process of surrender through confession, repentance, and acceptance of God's Grace through Jesus.

Understand you have sinned. We are all sinners.

Romans 3:23

For everyone has sinned;
we all fall short of God's glorious standard.

See that God's free gift is Eternal Life through Jesus.

Romans 6:23

For the wages of sin is death, but the free gift of God is
eternal life through Christ Jesus our Lord.

Trust that Jesus paid the penalty for your sin because He loves you.

Romans 5:8

But God showed his great love for us by sending Christ
to die for us while we were still sinners.

Confess and repent by declaring that Jesus is Lord and believe that God raised Him from the dead.

Romans 10:9-10

*If you openly declare that Jesus is Lord and believe
in your heart that God raised him from the dead,
you will be saved. For it is by believing in your heart
that you are made right with God, and it is by openly
declaring your faith that you are saved.*

Believe that God has saved you.

Romans 10:13

*For "Everyone who calls on the
name of the LORD will be saved."*

Pray this prayer: Heavenly Father, I trust your Word is
Truth. I surrender my sinful life to you. My sins lead to
death, but faith in your Son, Jesus, leads to eternal life. I
choose eternal life. I confess that I am not worthy and turn
from my sinful nature to accept the Grace you have offered
through Jesus. Please fill me with the power of your Spirit.
As a child of God, help me live a life pleasing to you, set
apart for your Glory. AMEN.

I praise Jesus for your decision now or before this.
I celebrate with the story of God's faithfulness in your
life. When we look at our lives through the lens of God's
faithfulness, it changes our perspective.

What is God's Faithfulness?

> Viewing our lives through the lens of God's faithfulness changes how we see ourselves and others.

Viewing our lives through the lens of God's faithfulness changes how we see ourselves and others. You may be wondering what I mean by God's faithfulness. I have talked about it a lot in this book. What is God's faithfulness? The Bible demonstrates God's faithfulness, but I want you to consider the following.

- It is the core of God's character. He is unchanging, dependable, and trustworthy. Psalm 100:5

- He is who He says He is and will do what He says He will do. Numbers 23:19

- His promises will not fail. Psalm 119:86

- He will never fail or abandon us. Deuteronomy 31:8

Have you taken the time to reflect on your life to identify the evidence of God's faithfulness? There may be times when you never thought to look for God's hand of protection or provision, but it was there. It is essential to recognize that God has been writing your story all along, even when you have not noticed.

The intentional focus on looking for and remembering God's faithfulness builds confidence in God and His ways. Another word for that confidence is faith. I remember a gentle question God would ask me repeatedly: "Do you have a full-time faith?" He asked me if I trusted Him for all my life. Do I believe He is faithful and worthy of my trust? Do I want to live fully surrendered, yoked to Jesus, or will I continue my yo-yo faith of trusting/not trusting, giving Him my concerns/picking them back up, pleasing Him on Sunday/living to please myself through the weekdays? Was I a Sunday plug-in to recharge, a part-time Christian, or was my desire to be connected to Him every day full-time? My desire was a full-time faith. I trusted God to show me what that looked like. I had marked His faithfulness throughout my life and wanted my life to reflect that.

> Yes, I want a Full-Time Faith! I want a God-centered life, not a Joni-centered life.

Yes, I want a Full-Time Faith! I want a God-centered life, not a Joni-centered life. The irony of a life consumed by depression is that everything I did was self-focused, while my deepest desire was to forget about myself, get out of my own way, and see the needs of others. You may be familiar with God's promise to His people following their captivity in Babylon in Jeremiah 29 to give them hope and a future. Still, the verses that follow are my favorite.

Jeremiah 29:12-14

*"In those days when you pray, I will listen. If you
look for me wholeheartedly, you will find me. I will
be found by you," says the LORD."*

Another picture of God's faithfulness. According to
these passages, a God-centered life prays, looks for God
wholeheartedly, and is found by a God who listens.

If you are ready to pursue a full-time faith, I recommend
reading *Experiencing God* by Henry and Richard Blackaby.[5]
He spends several chapters explaining how God reveals
His ways and speaks to His people. He covers how God
speaks through Scripture, prayer, the church, and our
circumstances. I saw in my own life the idea they share
that through our circumstances, God's invitation to join
Him in His work leads us to a crisis of belief. When I
read the chapters where the author explain this process,
it was an immediate connection. Let me share some of
their powerful insights, but please read the book and the
available study materials.

The author explains that a crisis is not a bad thing or
disaster as we often think when we hear it. It is a turning
point or a fork in the road that calls for us to decide what
we believe about God. The authors teach, "How you
respond when you reach this turning point will determine
whether or not you proceed with God in something only

5 Blackaby, H. T., Blackaby, R., & King, C. V. (2008). *Experiencing
God (2008 Edition): Knowing and Doing the Will of God, Revised and
Expanded*. B&H Publishing Group.

He can do or whether you continue on your way and miss what God has purposed for your life. This is not a one-time experience. How you live your life daily is a testimony of what you believe about God." They prepare the reader to understand that we will face a crisis of belief anytime God leads us to do something in a "God-sized" manner.

A crisis of belief would be dangerous if I lived a Joni-centered life. This is where the voice of the enemy, either myself or Satan, would mess with my mind saying, "Well, you don't have the faith you thought you did. You are an imposter, a hypocrite. How can you write a book about faith when you have a crisis of belief? How can you expect anyone to trust your experience when you are still walking it out?" Do you see the slippery slope? That is why we need to trust that what God says is true and not lean on our own understanding. (Proverbs 3:5-6)

Henry and Richard Blackaby suggest that a crisis of belief requires faith, adjustments, and obedience.

The authors suggest:

- Faith is the confidence that what God promised will come to pass, and if you can see that it can be easily done, then faith is probably not required.

- Faith is not found in our comfort zone.

- Faith must be centered on God himself and based on God's power, not human wisdom.

- Obedience, our actions show faith.

- What we do, not what we say we believe, reveals what we believe about God.

Consider the following Scripture on faith:

Hebrews 11:1 ESV

Now faith is the reality of what is hoped for, the proof of what is not seen.

2 Corinthians 5:7 ESV

For we walk by faith, not by sight.

1 Corinthians 2:4-5 ESV

[Paul said,] "My speech and my proclamation were not with persuasive words of wisdom, but with a demonstration of the Spirit and power, so that your faith might not be based on men's wisdom but on God's power."

Isaiah 7:9 NIV

If you do not stand firm in your faith, then you will not stand at all.

The second critical piece, according to Blackaby, is adjustments. The adjustments come as we align our viewpoint with God. Life adjustments will be needed because our ways are not His ways. (Isaiah 55:8-9) The gradual shift comes from working for God according to our abilities, gifts, and preferences to depending on God's work and resources. (John 15:5) Our surrender is total dependence on God.

Consider the following Scripture to understand what this surrendered life looks like.

John 15:5

"I am the vine; you are the branches. The one who remains in Me and I in him produces much fruit because you can do nothing without Me."

Galatians 2:20

I have been crucified with Christ, and I no longer live, but Christ lives in me. The life I now live in the flesh, I live by faith in the Son of God, who loved me and gave Himself for me.

Isaiah 41:10 HCSB

"Do not fear, for I am with you; do not be afraid, for I am your God. I will strengthen you; I will help you; I will hold on to you with my righteous right hand."

Isaiah 46:9-11

"I am God, and there is no other. ... My plan will take place, and I will do all My will. ... Yes, I have spoken; so I will also bring it about. I have planned it; I will also do it."

The authors of *Experiencing God* explain that we can follow God obediently as we make these adjustments. I must be honest with you at this point. Obediently following Jesus is terrifying for me because I know the person I am; I know my sinful thoughts and motives. I know that I can't do it on my own. Maybe you feel this way too. Often, we let our perspective of perfectionism prevent us from living the life God has called us to because we think we will never be able to meet His expectations. And who else is ready to jump on our bandwagon and reinforce the lie? Satan.

The whole point of faith is that we do what we do regardless of what we think or feel. When we love God, we desire to obey Him.

John 15:14-17, 21

Jesus tells His disciples, "If you love me, obey my commandments. And I will ask the Father, and he will give you another Advocate who will never leave you. He is the Holy Spirit who leads into all truth. The world cannot receive him because it isn't looking for him and doesn't recognize him. But you know him because he lives with you now and later will be in you. Those who accept my commandments and obey them are the ones who love me. And because they love me, my Father will love them. And I will love them and reveal myself to each of them."

1 John 4:9-10

"God showed how much he loved us by sending his one and only Son into the world so that we might have eternal life through him. This is real love—not that we loved God, but that he loved us and sent his Son as a sacrifice to take away our sins."

Be prepared for God to be all you need. He will move in your life like the most beautifully choreographed dance. You will find joy in suffering and strength in your weakness. He will ask you to trust, believe, adjust, and obey Him in every corner of your

> **Be prepared for God to be all you need.**

85

life. The result of this surrender and obedience is Full-Time Faith!

Dear One, what you believe about God changes everything. Ask yourself the questions I had to settle in my mind.

- Do you believe He is faithful and worthy of your trust?

- Do you want to live fully surrendered, yoked to Jesus?

- Do you have a yo-yo faith of trusting/not trusting, giving Him your concerns/picking them back up, pleasing Him on Sunday/living to please yourself through the weekdays?

- Do you attend church only on Sunday to plug in and recharge?

- Do you abide in Him every day – full-time?

It is time to WRAP Yourself in the Word. I will challenge you to look at several verses and intentionally seek the answers you need from God to help you see His faithfulness and have a Full-Time Faith.

WRAP each of the following verses. If you don't have the time to do them now, plan to do one verse for each of the following six days. I pray you will have increased confidence in God's faithfulness as you do this.

Psalm 100:5

For the LORD is good. His unfailing love continues forever, and his faithfulness continues to each generation.

Numbers 23:19

God is not a man, so he does not lie. He is not human, so he does not change his mind. Has he ever spoken and failed to act? Has he ever promised and not carried it through?

Deuteronomy 31:8

Do not be afraid or discouraged, for the LORD will personally go ahead of you. He will be with you; he will neither fail you nor abandon you.

Lamentations 3:22-23

The faithful love of the LORD never ends! His mercies never cease. Great is his faithfulness; his mercies begin afresh each morning.

Psalm 36:5

Your unfailing love, O LORD, is as vast as the heavens; your faithfulness reaches beyond the clouds.

Hebrews 13:8

Jesus Christ is the same yesterday, today, and forever.

WRAP Yourself in the Word

Write

Write the verse.

Psalm 100:5

Numbers 23:19

Deuteronomy 31:8

Lamentations 3:22-23

Psalm 36:5

Hebrews 13:8

Read

Read the verse.

1. Read it to yourself.
2. Read it out loud to yourself.
3. Read it to someone else.

Apply

Apply the verse.

Ask yourself, what do I learn about God in this verse?
What do I learn about myself? What is to be my response
to God's faithfulness?

Psalm 100:5

Numbers 23:19

Deuteronomy 31:8

Lamentations 3:22-23

Psalm 36:5

Hebrews 13:8

Pray.

Pray the verse.

Father, help me see your faithfulness in my current and past life. I want to know your unfailing love, your faithful love, your unchanging love. Help me build my confidence in what your Word says about you, not how I see the world in my circumstances. Help me understand deep in my heart and know that you will never leave me or fail to uphold your promises. You are the same yesterday, today, and forever. AMEN.

Growth Challenge

Schedule coffee or tea with a friend and share your faith stories. Be sure to include stories about your faith legacies and where you have found God to be faithful.

Chapter Seven

A Clean Heart

*I've frequently felt like a child trying
to dip all the water out of the ocean.
The grace of God is so inexhaustible
and, at times, overwhelming.*

Jerry Bridges, Transforming Grace

I was having tea with a friend, and she shared an experience from her Biblical Counseling session with me. She went to the session with a heavy heart unable to process much of what had happened in her life after a devastating change. She hesitated to go to the session that day, knowing she was not in a good place to handle the explosion of emotions nearing the top of her heart. She sat on the other side of the counselor's desk, listened, and took detailed notes. Eventually, the counselor stopped and asked if she was getting this. "Are you understanding God's grace? Do you understand what that means?"

With tears in her eyes, my friend shared her tender and surprising response. "I had asked for forgiveness all my life, but I had never accepted God's grace with the understanding that I was forgiven." My heart ached for her. She continued to be impacted by God's overwhelming kindness and mercy yet realized she had not shown kindness and mercy to herself. The idea that God pours blessings on us versus punishes us as we deserve is challenging because, most of the time, our life experiences do not support this basic concept of our faith as Christians. We fully expect to be punished or condemned.

Have you ever received God's grace? Don't be too quick to answer. Think about it. Have you asked for forgiveness all your life but never understood the magnitude of God's grace for you?

Thank you, God, that my relationship with you is based on the perfect sacrifice of Jesus and not my daily disappointing behavior. The freedom of knowing this vital message of the Gospel brings me great joy. It is also comforting when I need to acknowledge and deal with my sin. It is important to acknowledge our sinfulness even though we are forgiven through God's grace. We must deal with our sins and not be careless, thinking we have a free pass to be unrighteous. Our response to our sins should be like that of David.

> We must deal with our sins and not be careless, thinking we have a free pass to be unrighteous.

Psalm 51:10-12 ESV

Create in me a clean heart O God and renew a right spirit within me. Cast me not away from your presence and take not your Holy Spirit from me. Restore to me the joy of your salvation and uphold me with a willing spirit.

This passage of Scripture (that I committed to memory as a young woman) has comforted me and provided hope. God used it to deepen understanding of the Christian's responsibility toward sin. Let me explain this briefly. It's important for you to understand this statement as it relates to our maturity as Christians. It is foolish to think that, as a believer, you can throw the grace card down to cover your sins and choose to continue sinful behavior. Christians often cite 1 John 1:9, which says that if we confess our sins, God is faithful to forgive us. While this is the truth, it is not a free get-out-of-sin card that allows us to go on sinning.

Through the sacrifice of Christ on the cross, we have freedom from the power of sin and death. Yet, we will continue to be tempted to sin on this side of eternity. The Holy Spirit's job is one of conviction and compassion. He alerts us to our sins through the conviction of regret. It is our responsibility to recognize it and seek restoration through repentance. In his letter to the Christians in Rome, Paul explains that because we are dead to sin, we are alive in Christ, so we must not let sin control how we live. (Romans 6) Our response is to choose to do the things that lead to holiness. This is the process of Christian maturity, progressively becoming more like Jesus. This is our responsibility toward sin. In a later chapter, we will discuss the concept of sanctification (the process of Christian maturity) in more detail.

By digging deeper into Psalm 51, we can understand the condition of King David's heart, giving us a model for confession and repentance, which includes having regret, being willing to repent, and allowing God to restore our hearts.

Regret

What is regret? You know the "should have, would have, could have" or the "if only" of life. The emotion of feeling sad or disappointed over something that happened or didn't happen can lead to shameful anxiety and grief. We all experience regret. The world will tell you to live a life of no regrets or never live with regret, but learn from it, or regret is a waste of time. Is there some good reasoning behind these sentiments? Maybe, but as Christians, we must learn how to recognize and respond to regret. God does not want us to live in regret. 2 Corinthians 7:10 illustrates this comparison to Godly sorrow or worldly sorrow, which is regret. "For the kind of sorrow God wants us to experience leads us away from sin and results in salvation. There's no regret for that kind of sorrow. But worldly sorrow, which lacks repentance, results in spiritual death."

Psalm 51 is known as a Penitential Psalm because it is a prayer of confession written by King David following a reprimand from the prophet Nathan (2 Samuel 11-12). David had committed adultery with Bathsheba, and to cover it up, he ordered her husband's death, involving and corrupting others to carry out his instructions. Psalms 32 and 38, also Penitential Psalms written by David, are believed to be related to his deceptive circumstances with Bathsheba.

A commentary on Psalms 32, 38, and 51 suggests that David was a sick man. It seems guilt and remorse over his sins took a physical toll on King David. He had constant pain (Psalm 38:6, 51:8), he may have been dehydrated (Psalm 32:4), and he experienced heart problems, weakness, and blindness (Psalm 38:10).

While I don't believe all our suffering comes from disobedience and sin, I can tell you that I experienced physical pain and distress during my depression. I do not think my suffering was a punishment from God, and I fully accept the consequences of my choices. Like King David, I agonized over the guilt and shame and cried out to God for mercy

> The condition of the heart-stricken with guilt and shame can find comfort the same way King David did by crying out to God.

and forgiveness. I had deep regret over my thoughts and actions.

The condition of the heart-stricken with guilt and shame can find comfort the same way King David did by crying out to God.

Psalm 51:1-2

Have mercy on me, O God, because of your unfailing love. Because of your great compassion, blot out the stain of my sins. Wash me clean from my guilt. Purify me from my sin.

David knew the condition of the human heart and that only God could cleanse his heart. He needed his entire person to be cleansed. The regret over his sin was impacting his whole being. He desperately wanted restoration so he could be helpful to the Lord.

Repent

Repentance brings freedom, assurance, and confidence to our souls. We find freedom when we humble ourselves,

> Repentance brings freedom, assurance, and confidence to our souls.

trust God, and surrender all of the shame, brokenness, and guilt. However, our surrender requires us to know the content of our hearts. When we recognize the regret, we can be honest and allow God to search and reveal what is in our hearts. That is not easy to do. This kind of trust comes from knowing God, from hiding His truth in our hearts. (Psalm 119:11) What we know about God is tested, like our crisis of belief, when we have to confront our sin. Our heart is exposed and vulnerable when we bear our sins, but we are safe in God's tender mercy and grace.

I had to understand what was genuinely sinful and what were the lies I had come to believe about myself and my circumstances. Over time, I had allowed my circumstances to feed the lies and the stories I chose to believe about myself and the people closest to me. I believed the stories I replayed in my thoughts, even though they were untrue. Satan had been allowed access to my life through these faulty thoughts and emotions. He distracted me with lies from my past, creating confusion. He distorted the truth of my current situation while I tried to understand what was happening in my life. Satan's first tactic or strategy in our lives is often to bring discouragement. He will use what is familiar to us and twist the truth; we become so distracted that we fall into discouragement and, if not corrected, despair. Satan wanted me to believe that my sin was too much and that I could never recover. The power of the Holy Spirit through prayer revealed the truth to me.

When I approached Psalm 51, I desired a clean heart filled with the Holy Spirit and the joy of salvation. How would God provide that for me? Could the truth I had memorized in these verses be true for me?

Verses 10-12 were my prayer for many months. I recited them nightly, praying for a restful sleep free from devastating night terrors. Like King David, I was desperate for restoration.

Psalm 51:10 ESV

Create in me a clean heart, O God,
and renew a right spirit within me.

I wanted what King David wanted. A new heart. He knew only God could change his heart. I was learning that as well. Shortly after I started counseling and began healing, I enrolled in our Biblical Soul Care classes at church. Mostly, I sat in class every Sunday night and cried. Listening to the voice of Satan and "my committee" (aka voices in my head, my inner dialogue) saying, "How are you ever going to help someone else with soul care when you are such a mess yourself?"

Here is a glimpse of my healing: I love college and NFL football. Sunday afternoons and evenings were a coveted time for me. So, honestly, it was all about me. I reserved my Sunday afternoons and evenings for football. Our church had offered the soul care class for a few years, and I always thought it sounded like something I would like or should do. I was always looking for more to add to my plate. It was a coping mechanism that prevented me from dealing with the important stuff. Keeping me busy with too much is a favorite tactic of Satan to distract me. I never signed up for the class because it was only offered on Sunday nights. See the dilemma? No way was I missing football, so I never signed up.

Eventually, I attended an informational meeting after church one Sunday because I could be home for the 1:00 game. God used a few people in the ministry to convince me that I wouldn't miss too many games, and besides, one of the trainers was also a football fan and would be making the sacrifice, too. I started the class that September. And over time, missing football became pretty trivial to growing in the grace and knowledge of Jesus I experienced. (2 Peter 3:18) God can use the most trivial moments in our lives to move us toward Him. When we recognize Him move in the small matters of our lives, it gives us confidence in His faithfulness during hard times that seem like the big moments.

> When we recognize Him move in the small matters of our lives, it gives us confidence in His faithfulness during hard times that seem like the big moments.

Restore

God began to teach me about the condition of my heart and showed me how confession was a tool for cleansing my heart. Satan used my interests, like football, to keep me from what God wanted for me. But God has the final say over my life, and His Spirit led me to restoration.

Studying the heart through a Biblical lens, I learned that it is the center of our physical, mental, and spiritual lives and is connected to our thinking, feeling, and behavior. Later in the book, I share more and a few of the resources God used in my healing as I learned about the heart. God answered my prayer for a new heart.

Psalm 51:11 ESV

*Cast me not away from your presence
and take not your Holy Spirit from me.*

Why did King David pray this? Why did I pray this? I was fearful that God would not see anything worthy in me to restore. Again, it is a lie and a distraction from Satan. He used my flawed thinking to convince me that God was far from me and that I was not redeemable. I fully accepted God's grace but was not thinking clearly and was overly dependent on my thinking versus trusting in the Truth. Do you ever find yourself in this predicament? Trusting in your ways and not God's ways.

In 1 Samuel 15, God sent Samuel to anoint Saul as king over the people of Israel. Saul did not obey the instructions of the Lord, and God regretted anointing Saul as king. God sent Samuel to find a son of Jesse and anoint him as king. Samuel found David.

1 Samuel 16:13-14

Samuel took the horn of oil and anointed him in the presence of his brothers, and from that day on the Spirit of the LORD came powerfully upon David. Samuel then went to Ramah. Now the Spirit of the LORD had departed from Saul, and an evil spirit from the LORD tormented him.

That's why David prayed. He knew God withdrew His spirit from a disobedient Saul, and David feared the Lord would do the same to him. David was so profoundly tormented by sin that he prayed that God would not remove the Holy Spirit from him. David's heart differed significantly from Saul's, and God's blessings remained on David because of his repentant heart.

I prayed this because I knew the power of the Holy

> I did not want any of my sins to cause disobedience to God. Instead, I want a willing spirit surrendered to God.

Spirit as the presence of Jesus in me. God sent the Holy Spirit to believers at Pentecost under the new covenant with Christ. He is the Spirit of Truth, and He abides in us. (John 14:15-18, John 15:26) I did not want any of my sins to cause disobedience to God. Instead, I want a willing spirit surrendered to God.

Psalm 51:12 ESV

Restore to me the joy of your salvation
and uphold me with a willing spirit.

Confessing our sins is the first step. Next, we must surrender our hearts, minds, and wills to God and allow His Spirit to restore and renew us.

Romans 8:13-16

For if you live according to the flesh, you will die, but if by the Spirit you put to death the deeds of the body, you will live. All who are led by the Spirit of God are sons of God. You did not receive the spirit of slavery to fall back into fear, but you have received the Spirit of adoption as sons, by whom we cry, "Abba! Father!" The Spirit himself bears witness with our spirit that we are children of God.

Through this renewal, we are equipped with the Holy Spirit's power to overcome the slavery of sin. Will we still sin? Yes, but we are no longer slaves to the power of sin and death. Since the power of sin does not control us, we have a responsibility to deal with it properly. God is always faithful to forgive us. We are reassured in the following passage from 1 John.

1 John 1:8-9

If we claim to be without sin, we deceive ourselves and the truth is not in us. If we confess our sins, he is faithful and just and will forgive us our sins and purify us from all unrighteousness.

Thank you, Jesus!

Renewed with Hope

When I read verse 13 of Psalm 51, I felt known and loved by God. I have always been at my best when teaching and helping others learn, explore, and find God's truths. My favorite part of learning is teaching. Another example of God's faithfulness came after my confession and trusting God to renew and restore me.

Psalm 51:13

Then I will teach transgressors your ways so that sinners will turn back to you.

God could still use me, and I would be a more powerful testimony of His glory and faithfulness. I turned from my sin and turned toward God for renewal and restoration. My gifts and desires were still there, waiting to be ignited and unleashed. I was filled with hope for the first time in many years.

> My gifts and desires were still there, waiting to be ignited and unleashed.

Read them all together.

Psalm 51:10-13

Create in me a clean heart, O God,
and renew a right spirit within me.
Cast me not away from your presence,
and take not your Holy Spirit from me.
Restore to me the joy of your salvation,
and uphold me with a willing spirit.
Then I will teach transgressors your ways,
and sinners will return to you.

Reading Psalm 139, we know that God knows us; He searches our hearts and knows the word before it's even on our tongue. He knows our actions, where we go, our thoughts, and our motives. He is constantly with us. We cannot escape His presence. He designed our bodies and planned our days. He knows our strengths and weaknesses and wants to walk with and guide us. His plan is for our very best. Of course, God restored me and is using me to teach. Of course, God is using the gifts and abilities He gave me to bring glory to Him and His kingdom. That's how it works.

WRAP Yourself in the Word with Psalm 51:10-13.

WRAP Yourself in the Word

Write

Write the Word

Read

Read the Word

- Read it to yourself.
- Read it out loud to yourself.
- Read it to someone else.

Ask/Apply

Apply the Word

1. List the action words from David in this prayer.

2. Where do I need God's help applying this passage?

3. What is the promise David makes to God?

4. Can you make this promise?

Pray

Pray the Word

Father, create a clean heart and renew my strong faith in me. Please do not take the Holy Spirit from me or cast me away from your presence. Restore the joy of salvation to my clean heart. Help me boldly share your truth and grace with others so they will turn to you for salvation. AMEN.

Growth Challenge

Pray Psalm 139 back to God, pausing after each stanza, listening for God's response to you. Journal what you hear. Don't hear anything? Sit longer in silence or break the Psalm into shorter sections and concentrate on one part each day. Do this daily for a week and notice the changes in your thoughts.

Chapter Eight

Sit Walk Stand

If he is not sitting before God,
he cannot hope to stand before the Enemy.

Watchman Nee

I had a personal encounter with growing in holiness when I realized how God was working in my life with the gift of WRAP Yourself in the Word. God saw in me more than I saw in myself. He knew exactly the journey I would take. He knew that by growing roots established in His love, I would have the strength to understand and share His love with others. (Ephesians 3)

When I cried out for Him in my desperate prayer to be like the tree in Psalm 1:3, He knew how important it would be for me to abide in Him through delighting in His Word and meditating on it day and night. (Psalm 1:2). He knew my sanctification process would help me understand how the world works and where I needed to set myself apart from the wicked sinners and scoffers. (Psalm 1:1)

The fact that you are reading this book is further proof of God's faithfulness. You're reading a book that

> He brought Scripture to speak deeply to my purpose and identity in Him.

He planted in my heart years ago. He brought Scripture to speak deeply to my purpose and identity in Him. He led me through a gentle process of writing and reading His Word. And because you are reading it digitally or holding it physically, it is evidence that I was obedient to the Holy Spirit. Praise Jesus, from whom all blessings flow!

As I have described the process of each letter of WRAP in previous chapters, I would like to expand and connect the practice of Ask and Application with the idea of meditation. The primary point of meditation is application. The practice of meditation is simply thinking about God's Word and applying it to our lives. Meditation isn't just emptying the mind of all distractions and thoughts. Meditating on God's Word invites the Holy Spirit to transform your mind as you write, read, apply, and pray. It takes discipline, which is why WRAP Yourself in the Word is a powerful way to take in, meditate, and pray on God's Word.

In *The Pursuit of Holiness*, Jerry Bridges suggests a humble and consistent intake of the Scripture in the following ways.[6]

---

6 Bridges, Jerry, *The Pursuit of Holiness*. NavPress

1. Hearing the Word taught – Jeremiah 3:15
2. Reading the Bible ourselves - Deuteronomy 17:19
3. Studying Scriptures intently – Proverbs 2:1-5
4. Memorizing key passages – Psalm 119:11

Bridges also adds this caution, "But if we are to pursue holiness with discipline, we must do more than hear, read, study, or memorize Scripture. We must meditate on it. God said to Joshua, as he was assuming leadership over Israel, "Do not let this Book of the Law depart from your mouth; meditate on it day and night, so that you may be careful to do everything written in it" (Joshua 1:8). To meditate on the Scriptures is to think about them, turning them over in our minds, and applying them to our life's situations." Bridges encourages his readers that meditating on the Word of God is a practice developed through discipline. We may think we don't have time for meditation, but there are blocks of time during the day when the habit of meditation can be developed.

The blessings of meditating on God's instructions in Joshua include success and prosperity, similar to those in Psalm 1. Meditation leads to application, where we grow in Christlikeness through obedience.

In *Spiritual Disciplines for the Christian Life*, Donald S. Whitney says, "We think about what we delight in. According to Psalm 1, the result of such meditation is stability, fruitfulness, perseverance, and prosperity."[7] Whitney points out that promises for those who meditate

7 Whitney, D. S. (1991). *Spiritual Disciplines for the Christian Life*. http://ci.nii.ac.jp/ncid/BB14747876

on the Word continue from the Old Testament in the New and points to the assurance found in James.

James 1:22-25

But don't just listen to God's word. You must do what it says. Otherwise, you are only fooling yourselves. If you listen to the word and don't obey, it is like glancing at your face in a mirror. You see yourself, walk away, and forget what you look like. But if you look carefully into the perfect law that sets you free, and if you do what it says and don't forget what you heard, then God will bless you for doing it.

Whitney concludes that when our meditation leads to being "doers" of the Word, becoming more like Jesus, we will be blessed, "We have seen that as meditation leads to obedience, so obedience results in God's blessings like promises found in Psalm 1:3 and Joshua 1:8."

In his book, *Prayer*, Tim Keller says, "If prayer is to be a true conversation with God, it must be regularly preceded by listening to God's voice through meditation on the Scripture." He also suggests that meditation is a bridge that connects Bible study to prayer. Keller notes that Psalm 1 is a picture of meditation, "The person experienced in meditation is like a tree rooted so that wind cannot blow it away. Notice that this tree is planted by streams of water. Trees by streams do well even if there is little rain. This is an image of someone who can keep going in hard, dry times. We need to have the roots of our heart and soul in God at such times, and meditation is the way to do that."[8]

That was my cry:

Lord, I want to be like that tree. Plant me firmly by your living waters so my roots grow deep into your refreshing streams of truth. I will not thirst in drought because your living water is running through me. Father, create fruit in me to grow in the seasons you had established for me before I was born. Father, please don't let me wither. I do not want to be this way ever again. I want to be alive and flourish in what You have called me to do and created me to be. I never want to wither. Father, please let me prosper in all I do. I want my life to bring you Glory.

Meditation on God's Word was my answer. God answered this cry in several additional and incredible ways. He continued to draw me into understanding all He had for me in Psalm 1 and throughout the Bible. The more I delighted in His Word, the less I minded the gentle ways he molded my character through Christlike obedience.

In chapter five, I shared the process He asked me to consider as I evaluated my life according to where I was

> The more I delighted in His Word, the less I minded the gentle ways he molded my character through Christlike obedience.

8 Keller, T. (2014). *Prayer: Experiencing Awe and Intimacy with God.* Penguin.

walking, sitting, and standing with the wicked, sinner, or scoffer. While I didn't always like what this evaluation revealed, it did lead me to ask another question. How and where should I be walking, sitting, and standing? What would I replace the old with that would lead me to know more about who I was and what I was called to do? We see this idea of putting off or replacing the old and putting on the new in Ephesians.

Ephesians 4:22-24

Since you have heard about Jesus and have learned the truth that comes from him, throw off your old sinful nature and your former way of life, which is corrupted by lust and deception. Instead, let the Spirit renew your thoughts and attitudes. Put on your new nature, created to be like God—truly righteous and holy.

That one question led me to discover a small but mighty book by Watchman Nee. From 1923 to 1950, Nee founded 200 churches. In 1952, he was arrested, found guilty of false charges, and imprisoned until his death in 1972. The book *Sit Walk Stand: The Process of Christian Maturity* is an insightful and inspiring look at the truths found in Ephesians. Nee describes the process of Christian living and maturity in three words: sit, walk, and stand. God used this book to point me to His Truth and answer the questions of who I was and what I was called to do. Do you see the exact three words from Psalm 1?

Nee divides Ephesians into three parts:

1. Sit - Our Position in Christ (1:1-3:21)

2. Walk - Our Life in Christ (4:1-6:9)

3. Stand – Our Attitude to the Enemy (6:10-24)

Nee summarizes the book by saying, "God has made us to sit with Christ in the heavenly places, and every Christian must begin his spiritual life from that place of rest. In the second part, we select the word "walk" as expressive of our life in the world, which is its subject. We are challenged there to display in our Christian walk conduct that is in keeping with our high calling. And finally, in the third part, we find the key to our attitude toward the Enemy contained in the one word "stand" (6:11), expressive of our place of triumph at the end."[9]

Throughout the book, Nee repeats that our Christian experience begins with sitting, and our deliverance from sin is not something we do but rests on what God has done for us. "For no Christian can hope to enter the warfare of the ages without learning first to rest in Christ and in what He has done, and then, through the strength of the Holy Spirit within, to follow Him in a practical, holy life here on earth."

As he moves to the third part of the book, Nee explains that we put on the whole armor of God to stand against the evil one. "For our part, we need not struggle to occupy ground that is already ours. In Christ, we are conquerors—nay, "more than conquerors" (Rom. 8:37). In

---

9 Nee, Watchman. *Sit, Walk, Stand, The Process of Christian Maturity.* CLC Publications. Kindle Edition.

Him, therefore, we stand. So, we do not fight for victory; we fight from victory. We do not fight in order to win but because, in Christ, we have already won. Overcomers are those who rest in the victory already given to them by their God."

Reread that. As overcomers, we rest in the victory already given to us in Christ.

There is freedom in our position against the enemy, not to gain more ground but to stand in victory. This perspective helps when I feel myself sliding back into striving and working independently from God. Nee says we should not pray for God to enable us to overcome the Enemy but praise Him because He has already done so. Do you praise God and approach life from a place of victory as one who has overcome?

> When I hold God's Truths above my thoughts and feelings, Satan's grip on distorting the truth and other distracting tactics fades.

I love Nee's complete message in his book: "Only those who sit can stand. Our power for standing, as for walking, lies in our having first been made to sit with Christ. The Christian walk and warfare alike derive their strength from his position there. If he is not sitting before God, he cannot hope to stand before the Enemy."

I know one thing for sure: Satan was ill-prepared to come against the power of

God's Word as I continue to WRAP myself in the Word. When I hold God's Truths above my thoughts and feelings, Satan's grip on distorting the truth and other distracting tactics fades. I decide who is the boss of my mind daily. Who or what do I let have access to and influence my thoughts, emotions, and behaviors? Will I choose death and sin or life and Jesus? I began to sit with Christ, walk in the Spirit, stand before the Enemy, and fight from the victory Christ has already won for me.

WRAP Yourself in the Word

Write

Write the Word

Let's look at three anchor verses from Ephesians that Watchman Nee used in his book.

Ephesians 2:6

For he raised us from the dead along with Christ and seated us with him in the heavenly realms because we are united with Christ Jesus.

Ephesians 4:1

Therefore I, a prisoner for serving the Lord, beg you to lead a life worthy of your calling, for you have been called by God.

Ephesians 6:11

Put on all of God's armor so that you will be able to stand firm against all strategies of the devil.

Read

Read the Word

1. Read it to yourself.

2. Read it out loud to yourself.

3. Read it to someone else.

4. Read the verse in a different translation. The verses above are from the New Living Translation. Try the English Standard, ESV, or the New International Version, NIV.

Ask/Apply

Apply the Word

Ephesians 2:6

1. Is there a promise, instruction, or command in this verse?

2. Where do I need God's help applying them?

3. What is the most important thing God wants me to see and do in response to this verse?

Ephesians 4:1

1. Is there a promise, instruction, or command in this verse?

2. Where do I need God's help applying them?

3. What is the most important thing God wants me to see and do in response to this verse?

Ephesians 6:11

1. Is there a promise, instruction, or command in this verse?

2. Where do I need God's help applying them?

3. What is the most important thing God wants me to see and do in response to this verse?

Pray
Pray the Word

Father, Thank you for the gift of grace. Help me daily know that this gift is from you, and I don't need to work to achieve grace. Help me know that I have a place of rest, sitting with Jesus in the heavenly places. Father, show me through your Spirit and your Word exactly what that means to sit with Jesus. Help me walk a life filled with your Spirit to all you have called me to. Please help me understand what that looks like in my life. Your ways are not my ways, and sometimes I don't understand your ways. Help me, Father, stay disciplined in reading your Word with a spirit of wisdom and revelation to know you and walk in my calling as a Child of God. You have loved and chosen me, and I desire to be worthy of you. You have already won victory for me against Satan. Keep that a constant reminder in my heart, mind, and spirit as I encounter disappointment and discouragement. Please remind me to stand in victory. Help me be strong as I put on the whole armor of God—standing firm with the belt of truth and the body armor of righteousness. Help me fix my feet with shoes of peace from your Word. Help me hold up the shield of faith to repel the fiery darts from the Evil one. Secure me with the helmet of salvation as I use the sword of the Spirit, your Word of Truth, to defend the ground you have already won. I pray continually to live as an overcomer with words to boldly explain the mysteries of your Good News. In Jesus' name, AMEN

Growth Challenge

Consider how your daily life would change if you approached your circumstances and people from the perspective of victory as one who has overcome. Journal your thoughts, or better yet, have a deep, meaningful conversation about this perspective with a friend.

Chapter Nine

Guard Your Heart

Many people make the mistake of thinking
they can measure the certainty of
salvation by their feelings.

Corrie Ten Boom

Think back to the story of Adam and Eve, specifically to the encounter with the serpent. Bible translations call him the shrewdest or the craftiest of all creatures made. The crafty one didn't tempt Adam and Eve to murder, steal, or lie. He tempted them to doubt the Word of God.

Genesis 3:1

The serpent was the shrewdest of all the wild animals
the LORD God had made. One day he asked the
woman, "Did God really say you must not eat the fruit
from any of the trees in the garden?"

And then the serpent reels them into believing a big fatal lie.

Genesis 3:4-5

"You won't die!" the serpent replied to the woman. "God knows that your eyes will be opened as soon as you eat it, and you will be like God, knowing both good and evil."

Satan tempts them with the idea that they can be like God when they are already created in His image, enjoying the best God had for them. No, they didn't die immediately, but because of their actions, they would know death eventually.

Satan doesn't have any new tactics. He uses the same ones over and over again, and the crafty serpent will use the same tactics on you. We do not have to be vulnerable to Satan's lies or the doubts he plants in our hearts about God or ourselves. We can sit, walk, and stand in our position of victory. The more we sit with the Word and gain confidence in who we are in Christ and the deeper we walk in God's

> The more we sit with the Word and gain confidence in who we are in Christ and the deeper we walk in God's ways; the more Satan will desire to knock us off our game.

ways; the more Satan will desire to knock us off our game. He is the enemy. Although he does not win in the end, he will try to convince us otherwise. We need to be prepared for this by learning to guard our hearts. God's Word gives us instructions about the heart and directions on how to guard it from evil.

We are to guard the heart because the issues of our lives flow actively and continually from it. The Bible compares it to a spring that flows from the ground. Our lives are determined by what flows from our hearts. These passages remind me of the saying I used to tell my kids, and as adults, they often remind me of "garbage in – garbage out."

Proverbs 4:23

Guard your heart above all else,
for it determines the course of your life.

Matthew 12:34-35

For whatever is in your heart determines what you say.
A good person produces good things from the treasury
of a good heart, and an evil person produces evil things
from the treasury of an evil heart.

What about our heart makes it so powerful to direct our lives? God refers to something much more than the organ that pumps fresh, oxygenated blood through our bodies. Remember that Biblical Soul Care class I enrolled in at church? That led to completing coursework toward a lay certification in Biblical Counseling. In this chapter, I want to share what I learned about the heart and how God faithfully taught me to examine the content of my heart.

I am grateful to acknowledge a continuous thread of God's faithfulness throughout my life and this book. Remember, looking at our life through the lens of God's faithfulness changes our perspective. It also gives the confidence to trust God in deeper ways, leading to more significant healing. As I grow in Godliness, healing comes from trusting that God's ways are greater than mine. (Isaiah 55:8) The more I seek Him, He reveals more of Himself, and I trust Him more. (Jeremiah 29:13-14) My greatest healing was revealed as I began to understand the content of my heart. Surrendering my heart and trusting God to restore me came through understanding what God's Word said about my heart.

> Surrendering my heart and trusting God to restore me came through understanding what God's Word said about my heart.

The Heart

Through Biblical Counseling and studying God's Word, I learned that Scripture has much to say about the heart. The heart is considered the core of who we are. Sometimes, the Bible will use words like heart, inner being, mind, and spirit to refer to the inner self. This can be confusing. However, author Ken Baugh does a great job of simplifying this for us. He suggests that we think of our soul as a bucket containing our body, the material self, and our immaterial self, the heart. "The soul is the totality of what makes up who you are as a human being created in the image and likeness of God."[10] Baugh goes on to explain that God created us to live as integrated beings, and both aspects of our selves are involved in the process of Christ-formation or growing in Godliness. Our heart is the center of who we are. It is the place where God does the work to transform us into His likeness. It is the seat of our thoughts, emotions, and actions.

While we will dig into each part separately, Ken Baugh shares a helpful word picture of the three aspects of the heart in his book *Unhindered Abundance*. "These three dynamics of the heart work together much like the gears in a car transmission to drive behavior." We don't all have to be auto mechanics to get the picture Baugh is painting here. He is showing the connectedness of how our thoughts, emotions, and actions (will) work together. What I love the most about his analogy and workings of

10 Ken Baugh, *Unhindered Abundance: Restoring our Souls in a Fragmented World* (Colorado Springs, CO: NavPress, 2021

the heart is how he presents a fourth gear. For now, that is a surprise yet to come. Keep that picture of the gears turning together, each one impacting the movement of the others as we explore them according to God's Word.

Thoughts

> Throughout Scripture, we see the idea that thinking is connected to the heart.

Our mind involves our ability to reason, understand, and discern – think. It includes our beliefs and opinions. Throughout Scripture, we see the idea that thinking is connected to the heart.

The shepherds get the angelic news of Jesus's birth, and they hurry to Bethlehem and find the baby lying in the manger. They tell everyone what happened and what they saw. We are told in Luke 2:19 that Mary kept all these things she experienced in her heart and thought about them often.

The well-known passage in Hebrews reminds us of the power of God's Word to reveal our hearts' intentions.

Hebrews 4:12

For the word of God is alive and powerful.
It is sharper than the sharpest two-edged sword, cutting
between soul and spirit, between joint and marrow.
It exposes our innermost thoughts and desires.

132

When God observed His people in Genesis and their human wickedness, He saw that everything they thought or imagined was evil. (Genesis 6:5)

In the New Testament, we are told that Jesus can determine what is in men's hearts by knowing their thoughts.

Matthew 9:4

Jesus knew what they were thinking, so he asked them, "Why do you have such evil thoughts in your hearts?

Luke 9:46-47

Then his disciples began arguing about which of them was the greatest. But Jesus knew their thoughts, so he brought a little child to his side.

The Apostle Paul refers to thinking as a function of the heart when he encourages our practice of thinking.

Philippians 4:8

And now, dear brothers and sisters, one final thing. Fix your thoughts on what is true, and honorable, and right, and pure, and lovely, and admirable. Think about things that are excellent and worthy of praise.

Jeremy Pierre, author of *The Dynamic Heart in Daily Life*, summarizes the thinking heart. "The Biblical writers present people as thinking creatures. They reason and understand. They possess knowledge. They remember past situations, interpret them in the present, and project estimations of their future based on their own structures of plausibility. What people believe about the world determines how they interpret new information they receive as they live in it. The thoughts of people's hearts are of monumental importance to the trajectory of their lives."[11]

Emotions

> Emotions play an essential role in the heart. They motivate us and serve as a gauge of what we value.

The heart is where our desires and passions operate. Emotions play an essential role in the heart. They motivate us and serve as a gauge of what we value. They include our longing, desires, and hopes.

Love dwells in the heart.

---

11 Pierre, J. (2016). *The Dynamic Heart in Daily Life: Connecting Christ to Human Experience.* New Growth Press.

1 Peter 1:22

*You were cleansed from your sins when you obeyed the truth,
so now you must show sincere love to each other as brothers
and sisters. Love each other deeply with all your heart.*

Love for God comes from the heart.

Mark 12:30

*And you must love the LORD your God with all your heart,
all your soul, all your mind, and all your strength.*

Joy and sorrow are experienced in the heart.

John 16:22

*So you have sorrow now, but I will see you again; then you
will rejoice, and no one can rob you of that joy.*

The heart is the source of our desire.

Psalm 37:4

*Take delight in the LORD, and
he will give you your heart's desires.*

Hate, unfortunately, also takes root in the heart.

Leviticus 19:17

Do not nurse hatred in your heart for any of your relatives. Confront people directly so you will not be held guilty for their sins.

Jesus teaches.

Matthew 6:21

Wherever your treasure is, there the desires of your heart will also be.

> The heart represents what we trust most, love most, and hope in the most.

The heart represents what we trust most, love most, and hope in the most. What we treasure, what captures our imagination and captivates our desires, will also control our hearts for good or evil. Jeremy Pierre states that, like thoughts, people's affections and desires have a monumental impact on the trajectory of their lives.

Will (Action)

The will can encompass our intentions and choices. It is helpful to go back to a summary from Pierre's book to get an overview of the concepts of intent and choice known as the will. "The Biblical writers understand people to be moral agents capable of intent, decision, and choice. People intend certain purposes in their actions. They make decisions based upon the loyalties of their hearts. They resolve to accomplish certain things. They dedicate their efforts to certain ideals. People have active wills that direct their conduct. The intentions of people's hearts are also of monumental importance of their lives."[12]

We make countless decisions every day, and Scripture tells us that the intentions held deep in our hearts reveal the dedication of the heart.

Matthew 15:8
(a quote from the prophet Isaiah)

These people honor me with their lips,
but their hearts are far from me.

---

12 Pierre, J. (2016). *The Dynamic Heart in Daily Life: Connecting Christ to Human Experience.* New Growth Press.

Matthew 15:18-20

But the words you speak come from the heart—that's
what defiles you. For from the heart come evil thoughts,
murder, adultery, all sexual immorality, theft, lying, and
slander. These are what defile you.

Jeremiah 17:9-10

The human heart is the most deceitful of all things, and
desperately wicked. Who really knows how bad it is? But I,
the LORD, search all hearts and examine secret motives.

Our will directs our conduct, and if we use the analogy
from Baugh, we can easily imagine the gears of our
emotions and thoughts driving our actions. All three gears
connected parts of our hearts. How do we impact these
gears to move in concert with the truth in God's Word and
grow in Godliness?

Change the Heart

Collecting knowledge and trying to understand the heart
fed my unbalanced desire to know things and my false
belief that I need to understand everything to have control
over it. Knowledge was and can quickly become an idol
for me. The most important thing I learned about the
heart was that lasting, transformational change only comes
through God. Only the power of the Holy Spirit living in us

changes our hearts. Behavior modification can work in the short term but doesn't address the motivation, beliefs, or values that drive our choices. Wanting to change or pure willpower can also impact our lives temporarily, but it isn't sustainable. We must be willing to surrender our thinking, emotions, and actions through faith in the Word of God.

Without faith, it is impossible to please God. (Hebrews 11:6) Faith is an act of the Holy Spirit, and when Scripture is applied to our lives, it can conform us to the image of Christ (grow in Godliness). Our becoming like Christ takes place in the heart. Our heart is changed by transforming our thoughts, emotions, and actions. Yes, our hearts are multi-dimensional, but the Word of God transforms us through the power of the Holy Spirit. This is such an essential concept for us to understand.

> The most important thing I learned about the heart was that lasting, transformational change only comes through God. Only the power of the Holy Spirit living in us changes our hearts.

Say it out loud! "The Word of God transforms my heart through the Holy Spirit living in me!"

How does it happen, and what is our responsibility in this heart change?

We must work hard to live a life that honors our God-given blessings. Even though God has equipped us through His divine power, we are responsible for living in obedience through a disciplined effort to grow in the grace and knowledge of Christ. (2 Peter 3:18) We can do this by renewing our minds.

Romans 12:1-2

And so, dear brothers and sisters, I plead with you to give your bodies to God because of all he has done for you. Let them be a living and holy sacrifice—the kind he will find acceptable. This is truly the way to worship him. Don't copy the behavior and customs of this world, but let God transform you into a new person by changing the way you think. Then you will learn to know God's will for you, which is good and pleasing and perfect.

How do you think God transforms the way we think? Yes, through His Word.

Let's revisit Ken Baugh's analogy of the gears. Imagine three gears, thoughts, emotions, and will drive our hearts. Gears are wheels with teeth, and the teeth on one gear fit in between the teeth on the gear beside it to cause movement. This picture helps us understand the working relationship between our thoughts, emotions, and will. They are interconnected and work together. Also, imagine the thought gear is bigger than the other two.

Spoiler Alert! Here comes the idea of the fourth gear. A much smaller gear that has the potential to move the thought gear and impact the other two gears, our emotions, and our will. Baugh suggests that this fourth gear can work for us or against us depending on what we allow it to represent. The gear can represent truth, God's Word, or lies. What we choose to believe drives this mighty, smaller fourth gear and has the potential to drive all the other gears.

Here is how Baugh explains it. "Of the four gears, the only one we can directly control long term is Gear #1: Thoughts. With my thoughts, I can choose the fourth gear. I can decide if I will think thoughts based on God's truth or Satan's lies. Exercising our free will in regard to thoughts reveals how thinking directly affects how we live."[13]

Think back to the story of Adam and Eve being first deceived by the serpent. First, the crafty one caused them to think about what God said. The distortion began with a lie, which directed Eve's thoughts and impacted the gear of her emotions. The lie triggered Eve's desire to be like God, knowing good and evil. The connected gears turned, impacting the action of eating the fruit. The input of the thought of doubt was faulty, leading to unholy desires and resulting in an action to cover themselves and hide from God. (Genesis 3:7-8)

Paul commands us in Colossians 3:2 to "think about things of heaven, not the things of earth."

---

13 Ken Baugh, *Unhindered Abundance: Restoring our Souls in a Fragmented World* (Colorado Springs, CO: NavPress, 2021

Let this truth from Romans 8 wash over your thoughts. Receive these words with love and encouragement to understand that we can overcome our thoughts.

Romans 8:1-2

So now there is no condemnation for those who belong to Christ Jesus. And because you belong to him, the power of the life-giving Spirit has freed you from the power of sin that leads to death.

Romans 8:5-6

Those who are dominated by the sinful nature think about sinful things, but those who are controlled by the Holy Spirit think about things that please the Spirit. So, letting your sinful nature control your mind leads to death. But letting the Spirit control your mind leads to life and peace.

What I learned about the heart brought deep awareness about my thoughts. I wrestled with hard questions like:

- Where did these thoughts come from?
- How did I believe this for so long?
- Why didn't I see this?
- Who am I?
- What do I do now?

So many of my deeply rooted thoughts came from years of shame, false beliefs, striving, and faking it – my life was on autopilot.

In the following chapters, we will dive into what I learned about the fourth gear and how I changed and continue to evaluate the origin of my thoughts—first, a word of caution.

You are not me, so do not compare my transformation with where you are now. I still don't always have it figured out. Becoming more like Jesus is called progressive sanctification for a reason. This is not a quick healing fix or an "if I did it, so can you" pep talk. It is a prayerful commitment of obedience in faith. Your choice to examine and deal with the influences over your thought life will take deep introspection, prayer, a willingness to be wrong, and the courage to trust our loving, faithful God to change your heart.

> Your choice to examine and deal with the influences over your thought life will take deep introspection, prayer, a willingness to be wrong, and the courage to trust our loving, faithful God to change your heart.

He will get rid of the old and replace it with the new through His active and living Word.

We are taught in Ephesians the concept of "put off" and "put on." We will dive into this practically in the following chapters. Hear what God's Word says.

WRAP Yourself in the Word
Ephesians 4:22-24

Since you have heard about Jesus and have learned the truth that comes from him, throw off your old sinful nature and your former way of life, which is corrupted by lust and deception. Instead, let the Spirit renew your thoughts and attitudes. Put on your new nature, created to be like God—truly righteous and holy.

Write

Write the Word

Write the passage above from Ephesians.

Read
Read the Word

1. Read it to yourself.

2. Read it out loud to yourself.

3. Read it to someone else.

Ask/Apply
Apply the Word

- List the promises, instructions, or commands in this passage.

- What is the most important thing God wants me to see in this passage?

- Is there any unconfessed sin I need to talk to God about?

- Where do I need God's help responding to this passage?

Pray
Pray the Word

Father, I am created in your likeness in true righteousness and holiness. Your Word tells me I am a new creation because of my faith in Christ. Father, help me live with this truth. Renew my mind to think rightly of who I am when I am confronted with lies that I have chosen to believe and the destructive lies of Satan. Holy Spirit, replace the doubt with the truth that I can overcome the old and live new - created in God's image. Renew my thoughts and attitudes to think correctly about who you are and who I am in Christ. Help me focus on your truth, not lies that can easily be my default. Let your truth dwell boldly in my mind and heart. Father, let my actions shine the light of your truth to others. Let your Word transform me as I surrender. AMEN.

Growth Challenge

Ask God to show you where your sinful nature controls your thoughts and feelings and where He would like you to allow the Spirit to control your mind. Listen, journal, and talk to a friend who can help you with accountability.

Chapter Ten

Who's The Boss of Your Mind?

*Change your thoughts
and you can change your world.*

Norman Vincent Peale

I pray this chapter becomes a resource you repeatedly return to for encouragement. Before we go on, I need you to do a heart check. If you have not settled the following truths in your heart, you will need to go back to the beginning of this book and WRAP Yourself in God's Word until you can say yes, I agree, to these three positions of the heart.

1. I believe Jesus is God's son sent to redeem my sins. Jesus walked this earth and died, and his resurrected body proves that He will come again to reunite us with the Father when He establishes His kingdom for eternity.

> I trust that God's Word has the power through the Holy Spirit to transform my heart.

2. I trust that God's Word has the power through the Holy Spirit to transform my heart.

3. I believe I am a child of God through the gift of God's grace.

I also want to be clear on the concept of sanctification. At the moment of our salvation, when we first believed, we were accepted or justified by God. We received the Holy Spirit, which began making us more like Christ, our progressive sanctification. When Christ returns for the Church, we will live with Him eternally. This will be our glorification. See the outline below:

1. Justification (Past)—God declares us righteous when we believe in Jesus through faith. We receive Christ's righteousness and are found not guilty in God's sight.

2. Sanctification (Present) – God transforms us into Christ's image through the Holy Spirit's work. It is progressive work as we grow spiritually or grow in the Lord. This happens as a result of obedience to God's Word.

3. Glorification (Future) – We will be given a new resurrected body and live eternity with God when Jesus returns.

A passage I love as much as Psalm 1 is found in 1 John 3:1-3 and shows us all three aspects of our salvation.

1 John 3:1-3

See how very much our Father loves us, for he calls us his children, and that is what we are! But the people who belong to this world don't recognize that we are God's children because they don't know him. (Justification) *Dear friends, we are already God's children, but he has not yet shown us what we will be like when Christ appears. But we do know that we will be like him, for we will see him as he really is.* (Glorification) *And all who have this eager expectation will keep themselves pure, just as he is pure.* (Sanctification)

Our Sanctification – Growing in Godliness

The road map we will use to understand how to surrender our hearts begins with a foundational understanding that God accomplishes it. At the same time, we are responsible for participating in our sanctification.

1. **Faith:** We covered the topic of faith in a previous chapter when we looked at Full-Time Faith. The key is remembering that our faith is a gift through God's grace and where we begin all transformation and healing. There is an additional resource for you to use to prioritize your faith in the book's resource section. You will find this FAITH Map bonus by scanning the QR code or going directly to the website. FAITH is an acronym for Faithfulness, Abide, Instruction, Thankful, Hope.

2. **Thoughts:** Trusting God to reveal the contents of our hearts will bring awareness to our thoughts (Proverbs 3:5) and allow us to:

   - Recognize where they come from.

   - Respond to them in the right way.

   - Redeem them through God's Word.

   - Remain in fellowship with Christ.

3. **Surrender:** The antidote for striving is surrender. As God reveals the content of our hearts through our thoughts, emotions, and actions, we put off our way and put on His way. We respond by acting in obedience to His Word. (Proverbs 3:6)

   > The antidote for striving is surrender.

4. **Abide:** Learning to abide, we become like the believer, symbolized by the tree in Psalm 1 – blessed, delighted in

God's Word, rooted, fruitful, steadfast, and prosperous. Our abiding becomes the evidence – the fruit- of our salvation. We learn to obey, love God, love others, pray, and live joyfully. (John 15)

The Current State of My Heart

Honestly, I am struggling to complete the last few chapters of this book. I was on the phone with a friend last night when my husband overheard me tell her that I sure hope God doesn't plan another book for me. He later asked me why I said that. I fired this response with a tone, noting that he couldn't possibly understand what I was feeling. "Because that is how I feel right now. I am discouraged and disappointed in myself. It is too hard." The following day, before I was focused on seeing anything, he was ready to start his early day and asked if I was feeling better. I took the time to breathe and believe the best in him but quietly said, "We'll see." I gave him a hug and kiss before he left. As he was leaving, he reminded me that I could do this. I was brilliant, and he believed in me. "God placed a dream in your heart. He will give you the strength to accomplish it. Just trust Him."

His encouragement was sweet, and it felt good. I wanted more. I sent an SOS

> "God placed a dream in your heart. He will give you the strength to accomplish it. Just trust Him."

153

text out to my prayer warrior girlfriends. I was wrestling with the very subject I needed to write about. Oh, the ugly thoughts that crowded my mind and stirred my emotions. I was striving in my power and not trusting God for the outcome. Here is the text I sent.

"Would you please pray for me? I am trying to write the last few chapters of my book. I've been trying for the last three months. And it has been so hard. I've thought about giving up. There are many worthy distractions in my life, like trying to finish this house and a strategy for moving in: my grandkids, family, and everything I love dearly. The last few chapters are about how God used His Word and His influence to heal my heart, specifically my thinking and emotions. And, of course, that's where I'm having the most difficult time – between Satan, my lies, and thoughts that ruminate through my brain - I'm just discouraged, and I need Extra prayer. It has to be done in 3 days."

Now, here is the God part. None of them knew the content I was trying to write about, but God did. Here are a few of their prayer responses. I pray you have prayer warriors you can go to in your life. The God-appointed kind that helps you out of the pit and doesn't just commiserate with you or criticize your lack of faith. Write their names in the margin of this book. Text them after reading these prayers and share what you need.

"Yes, I absolutely will stop and pray for that for you! I mean, that last part that you just described is the very thing the enemy would like to silence. We overcome by the Blood of the Lamb and the word of our testimony!" Revelation 12:11

"I'm praying that the Spirit of the Lord would move in power in you and through to the pen what He wants communicated. Nothing more. Nothing less. His words. His thoughts. I pray that you will be able to quiet your mind (sound mind - 2 Timothy 1:7) and allow Him to flow through your mind. We can work from a place of REST. No striving. Just following the Spirit as He leads. Step by Step. Word by Word."

"Dear Lord, I am asking today for you to bring your destiny to Joni, give her the strength to believe in herself, and take all the negative discouragement thoughts from her mind. Free her mind from the insecurities, fears, and anxieties she is bound to. Let her hear your voice and your words today and every day. Remind her to fear not - you are always with us. Remind her also that you are her God.

Do not let Satan convince her that her worries are too big and cannot be solved. Help her fight. Refresh her and let her know that you didn't say, "Be strong if you feel like it"; you said to be strong and of good courage. We know that if we are not strong and courageous, the devil will creep in and overpower us. He puts the spirit of fear on us. Today, let her start thinking strongly, bravely, and courageously.

Let her do all things through Christ, who strengthens her. Today, Lord, renew her thoughts and let her know that she may not feel strong and courageous, but that doesn't mean that she isn't, for when she is weak, Lord, you are strong. Lord, your strength is perfect in weakness. In Jesus' name, I pray, amen."

There were more who called and prayed with me. I knew I had to make room in this chapter to share this moment. One thing God has made clear to me over the last two years as I wrote this book is to be transparent and share the truth of my healing. I don't have it all figured out, and I never want my words to discourage you. I am cheering for you. I am shaking my pom poms, yelling in the megaphone, and jumping up and down with excitement for you. I know what our God can do. He can do it for you, too. I pray you will take the time to connect with me either on my website or social media. The QR code in the resource section will help you find all the resources mentioned in the book and guide you to join my mailing list. I can't wait to meet you and rejoice and pray together.

Who's the Boss of Your Mind?

Who is the boss of your mind? That is the question. If you're like me, it depends on the circumstances. What if I told you that we can maintain a controlled thought life? Below, I share the strategies God helped me develop to gain control of my rambling, raging, and relentless thought patterns. This chapter is about practical strategies.

Fundamental foundational truths to consider:

- **Satan will use your thoughts and circumstances to distract you and distort the truth.** I call them tactics of distraction or "distractics." They are evil and never meant for good.

- **We choose what we think about.** This may seem radical if you have lived with your thoughts on autopilot for some time. It did to me.

- **We believe what we tell ourselves, even if it is untrue.** Think about the thoughts you have believed about yourself that come from you.

- **We don't have to believe lies.** We can filter them through the truth in God's Word and find freedom.

Strategy 1: Recognize and Respond Thought Inventory

How do you know what you think about? That may seem like a silly question because, after all, they are your thoughts. How often have you asked yourself, "What was I thinking?" I am challenging you to notice your thoughts. Use your WRAP journal or any journal or go to the resources on my website and download the free *Thought Inventory Journal* and track your thoughts.

For the next five days, pick a segment that includes a weekend day; notice your thoughts. On the first day, pray that God will bring awareness to your thoughts. For the next four days or more, track your general thoughts every 30 minutes. You may have blocks of time when you are doing something that captures your attention and you are focused. That's great. I challenge you to notice when your mind is wandering, unfocused, judgmental, bossy, and (in general) uncontrolled. When you log your thoughts, note any strong emotions, circumstances, and people.

After the five days, note patterns of emotions, thoughts, and lies you believe and repeat to yourself.

Surrender these and ask God to help you know what to do next. If you are concerned and alarmed by what your thoughts reveal, I suggest you talk to someone about them – a mature friend, pastor, or counselor.

Identify someone in your life you trust to do this activity with. This person can help you choose what to do next and keep you accountable.

Can you identify the origins of the thoughts? Do they come from your past family or childhood, cultural background, or life experiences?

How about any lies you identified? Are they connected to your past experiences or things you repeatedly tell yourself?

Remember, we have the power to choose our thoughts. We can decide what we think about and allow them to control us.

Ken Baugh addresses this concept in his book. "Whatever we choose to focus our mind on consistently becomes dominant in our mind, directly influencing our feelings and behavior. This helps us understand the correlation between thinking and Christ-formation. We can literally replace the lies and distorted thoughts that wreak havoc in our lives by replacing them with thinking that is aligned with the Bible. Focused attention on biblical truth results in freedom and abundance. Neuroplasticity can be self-directed by changing what we think about."[14]

Researcher, communications pathologist, and audiologist Dr. Caroline Leaf has worked in cognitive neuroscience for nearly four decades and describes what happens in our brain as we think: "As we think, we change the physical nature of our brain. As we consciously direct our thinking, we can wire out toxic patterns of thinking and replace them with healthy thoughts. New thought networks grow. It all starts in the realm of the mind, with our ability to think and choose."[15]

---

14 Ken Baugh, Unhindered Abundance: *Restoring our Souls in a Fragmented World* (Colorado Springs, CO: NavPress, 2021, 86
15 Caroline Leaf, *Switch on Your Brain: The Key to Peak Happiness,*

Strategy 2: Redeem and Remain

The Bible tells us that we wage war against the spiritual realm when we battle our thoughts.

2 Corinthians 10:3-5

We are human, but we don't wage war as humans do. We use God's mighty weapons, not worldly weapons, to knock down the strongholds of human reasoning and to destroy false arguments. We destroy every proud obstacle that keeps people from knowing God. We capture their rebellious thoughts and teach them to obey Christ.

Dr. Leaf reminds us of the power of our thoughts. "If you allow a thought to take root in your head, if you give it energy by thinking about it on a daily basis, it can spread, just like "a little yeast" in a lump of dough. Slowly but surely, this thought can impact your behavior and negatively influence your community. It can spread like a virus, and before you know it, your whole life can take a turn for the worse. Taking your thoughts captive should not, therefore, be optional. It is something that you should practice every moment of every day. Remember, no thought is harmless, and no attitude can be hidden."[16]

Will you commit your thoughts to God and trust Him for transformation? Consider what God spoke through

Thinking, and Health (Grand Rapids, MI: Baker Books, 2013), 20
16 Leaf, C. (2018). *Switch On Your Brain Every Day: 365 Readings for Peak Happiness, Thinking, and Health*. Baker Books.

Moses to the people of Israel about the choice of life or death; these instructions apply to us today. The critical issue to see here is that we have a choice.

Deuteronomy 30:19-20

Today I have given you the choice between life and death, between blessings and curses. Now, I call on heaven and earth to witness the choice you make. Oh, that you would choose life so that you and your descendants might live! You can make this choice by loving the LORD your God, obeying him, and committing yourself firmly to him. This is the key to your life.

As you prepare to surrender your thoughts for God to redeem, keep in mind the relationship of our thoughts, emotions, and actions. Dallas Willard writes that feelings and thoughts always go together. They are interdependent. "And just as thought and feeling are inseparable, so volition (will) is closely intertwined with them. To choose, one must have some object or concept before the mind and some feeling for or against it. There is no choice that does not involve both thought and feeling. On the other hand, what we feel, and think is (or can and should be), to a very large degree, a matter of choice in competent adult persons, who will be very careful about what they allow their mind to dwell upon or what they allow themselves to feel.[17]

---

17 Willard, Dallas. *Renovation of the Heart: Putting on the Character of Christ* (p. 34). The Navigators. Kindle Edition.

> Transformation comes when we act against our thoughts and align them with the truth of God's Word.

Transformation comes when we act against our thoughts and align them with the truth of God's Word. When we filter our thoughts or lies through the lens of God's truth, they become evident for what they are. We bring them into the light and can see Satan's distortion and distractics to confuse and condemn us.

Below are Scripture passages that will get you started. I did not include the words to these verses on purpose. Please look them up. WRAP them. Meditate on them.

John 17:17 NLT

*Make them holy by your truth;
teach them your word, which is truth.*

John 17:17 ESV

Sanctify them in the truth; your word is truth.

Romans 12:1-3
Proverbs 4:23

Isaiah 26:3
Colossians 3:1-17
Philippians 4:6-9
Ephesians 4:20-24
2 Timothy 3:14-17

Remember that Jesus lives in you and receives you just as you are. You do not have to have your mess all cleaned up for Him to transform you. When God looks at you, He sees you through the lens of Jesus. It is as if Jesus stands between you and God's sight

> When God looks at you, He sees you through the lens of Jesus.

line of you. Remember what David says in Psalm 139 about God's infinite mind compared to man's limited mind.

Psalm 139:17-18

How precious are your thoughts about me, O God. They cannot be numbered! I can't even count them; they outnumber the grains of sand! And when I wake up, you are still with me!

One last word about the transformative healing God's Word accomplished in me. I am different, but my greatest blessing has been how much difference it made in my relationships. It was hard work. It still is. My family had become used to relating to me in my brokenness. When my heart began to change, they witnessed different thinking patterns and the change in my attitudes and behaviors.

> Our relationships change when we change our thinking, and God begins to transform our hearts.

Our relationships change when we change our thinking, and God begins to transform our hearts. Thank you, Jesus! I would love to hear from you if you have found this to be true for you. Please message me through social media or contact me on the website. I want to hear your story.

WRAP Yourself in the Word

Write

Write the Word

Which passage will you write? All of them? Ok, let's do it. At the end of the book, you will find a list of Scripture I use in each chapter. Pick one or two from this chapter or choose a different chapter. I challenge you to spend each of the five days of your thought inventory with a different verse. I encourage you to use the passage that my friend prayed over me.

2 Timothy 1:7 (NKJV)

For God has not given us a spirit of fear, but of power and of love and of a sound mind. The NLT uses the words self-discipline in place of sound mind. The original Greek word speaks to the idea that we are called to our senses, to a sound mind with divine moderation and self-control.

Read

Read the Word

1. Read it to yourself.

2. Read it out loud to yourself.

3. Read it to someone else.

Ask/Apply

Apply the Word

- List the promises, instructions, or commands in this passage.

- What is the most important thing God wants me to see in this passage?

- Is there any unconfessed sin I need to talk to God about?

- Where do I need God's help responding to this passage?

Pray

Pray the Word

The prayer for this chapter is based on 2 Timothy 1:7. Father, thank you for not giving me a fearful and weak spirit. You have given me the power and resources to face every trial. Help me remember what I have been given and not trust the lies I tell myself or Satan's lies to distract me. I have the power of love. I can focus on pleasing you and others because of this love. Your Word tells me I have been given a sound mind. I claim that truth over my life and choose to live in the power of a self-controlled mind. I can live with wisdom and confidence in my power as a child of God. I surrender my mind, thoughts, and feelings to you. I trust you to redeem them and direct my life for good. AMEN.

Growth Challenge

Check out the FAITH Map on my website. Remember, you can easily access it using the QR code in the resource section of this book. You can use this tool in many ways: Bible Study, self-coaching, and evaluating where your Faith needs strengthening. Begin to consider: Where has God been faithful? What are your habits of abiding? How do you receive God's instruction? How do you express thankfulness? Where do you place your hope for today or the future?

Chapter Eleven

Surrender Your Striving

*The truth is that faith and obedience
are two sides of the same coin and
are always found together in the Scriptures.*

AW Tozer

I left a job that I deeply loved. I experienced wild success, and my team was nationally recognized for the content we created and delivered to help save lives in our state and across the country. I thought I was part of a team dedicated to the truth and overcoming obstacles to save lives. It was a complete lie. One side of the company had a specific agenda, and my public side had been working on different premises. I was devastated and left because I was unwilling to compromise the work to please people more powerful than me.

I know that sounds so righteous of me. Sort of. My pride was damaged, and I thought my reputation would be tarnished. I left for selfish reasons, albeit good reasons. What followed was a realization that my success enabled many things in my life that I no longer had access to, including travel, great friends, community impact, collaboration, and the pride of making a difference. The result was a broken person who tried to cover up the hurt. Striving to replace the financial income, my family's unique opportunities to do incredible things and meet cool people, and my reputation as a successful, confident professional led to more brokenness.

My striving led to poor decisions fueled by toxic thoughts and uncontrolled emotions. I believed the lies and expectations I had created for myself and what I thought everyone else expected of me. These lies and expectations almost killed me. But God! The last two steps on the sanctification road map, surrender and abide, are personal journeys to me. Maybe that is why the devil fought so hard against me sharing them with you.

> I learned faith was acting in obedience regardless of my thoughts or feelings.

One of my most profound areas of healing came when I was able to make the connection between my thoughts, emotions, and actions. I learned faith was acting in obedience regardless of my thoughts or feelings. I had to obey the knowledge I had gathered, leading me to Proverbs. This book is categorized as wisdom literature for good reason. God's instruction in Proverbs 16 gave me a deeper understanding of wisdom. Knowledge is gathered through study, but wisdom is the power to act on that knowledge. We are instructed to value wisdom.

Proverbs 16:16

*How much better to get wisdom than gold
and good judgment than silver!*

If you are up for a challenge. Set a goal for the next 33 days: WRAP each verse in Proverbs 16.

What my striving revealed about my heart was that I had obtained and valued knowledge, but I was a fool in applying the knowledge. I lacked wisdom. I lacked the trust and faith to walk in a manner worthy of my calling. (Ephesians 4:1) You can understand why God led me through Psalm 1 the way He did.

Before we proceed, let's define "striving" so we have a shared meaning and understanding. The consensus on dictionary meanings is that striving devotes serious effort or energy to something and can also be a struggle in opposition. It is something we try hard to do or achieve. The root word in Hebrew figuratively means to *wrangle* or *defend*.

While there is good striving when motivated for the correct reasons and desires, the Bible often offers instruction and wisdom against striving. Striving to achieve anything we are trying to do solely on our own with an attitude of self-reliance versus surrendering and trusting God will produce negative outcomes in our lives. This is the striving we are warned against in Scripture. The condition of a striving heart is filled with doubt about what to believe and some unbelief about God's power to intervene in the situation. The antidote for striving is surrender. Surrender involves trust and having faith that God is always for us.

The prophet Jeremiah demonstrated this trust and faith in the Lord. Jeremiah was called to speak to the leaders of Judah, who were more likely to trust their political partners than the power of God. He compares the leaders in Judah to a desert bush and the righteous way of the Lord to a fruitful tree by the water. The leaders' flawed thinking was leading the entire nation to destruction.

Jeremiah 17:5-6

This is what the LORD says: "Cursed are those who put their trust in mere humans, who rely on human strength and turn their hearts away from the LORD. They are like stunted shrubs in the desert, with no hope for the future. They will live in the barren wilderness, in an uninhabited salty land."

Jeremiah 17:7-8

"But blessed are those who trust in the LORD and have made the LORD their hope and confidence. They are like trees planted along a riverbank, with roots that reach deep into the water. Such trees are not bothered by the heat or worried by long months of drought. Their leaves stay green, and they never stop producing fruit."

The nation of Judah had turned away from God. The Wiersbe Bible Commentary describes the situation: "The heart of every problem is the problem in the heart, and the human heart is deceitful and incurable. God searches the

> God searches the heart and mind and knows how to reward each person.

heart and mind and knows how to reward each person. If we want to know what our hearts are like, we must read the Word and let the Spirit teach us."[18]

This is a drastic comparison of a simple choice. Trust or not trust. But aren't we faced with this essential decision over and over? How do we choose? The next verse tells us why the leaders and why we don't always trust God.

Jeremiah 17:9-10

"The human heart is the most deceitful of all things, and desperately wicked. Who really knows how bad it is? But I, the LORD, search all hearts and examine secret motives. I give all people their due rewards, according to what their actions deserve."

I acknowledge that my heart is not all that different than the Hebrews mentioned in Jeremiah, but the difference for you and me is Jesus. We live on this side of God's new covenant. We are washed with forgiveness through the

18 Wiersbe, W. W. (2007). *Wiersbe Bible Commentary NT.* David C Cook.

blood of Jesus. Think about how Wiersbe describes the problem. Essentially, our problems aren't the problems. It is how we respond in our hearts, how our thoughts and feelings direct our actions. God searches our hearts and knows the secret motives, yet through His mercy, we don't get what we deserve.

I would love to camp in Jeremiah's picture of the tree, but I will move on because we have some practical work to consider.

How to Surrender

I know I am striving when I sense some imbalance or uneasiness. It usually comes from people pleasing or an influence I have allowed on my heart, like the lies I believe about my identity in Christ or my God-given value. All of these distortions contribute to my striving. I continue to ask God to show me and help me become aware of my striving and where I need to surrender, repent, and rejoice in His forgiveness. Scripture tells us we can go to Him, and He will examine our anxious ways.

Psalm 139:1-12, 23-24

O LORD, you have examined my heart
and know everything about me.
2 You know when I sit down or stand up.
You know my thoughts even when I'm far away.
3 You see me when I travel
and when I rest at home.
You know everything I do.
4 You know what I am going to say
even before I say it, LORD.
5 You go before me and follow me.

You place your hand of blessing on my head.
6 Such knowledge is too wonderful for me,
too great for me to understand!
7 I can never escape from your Spirit!
I can never get away from your presence!
8 If I go up to heaven, you are there;
if I go down to the grave, you are there.
9 If I ride the wings of the morning,
if I dwell by the farthest oceans,
10 even there your hand will guide me,
and your strength will support me.
11 I could ask the darkness to hide me
and the light around me to become night—
12 but even in darkness I cannot hide from you.
To you the night shines as bright as day.
Darkness and light are the same to you.

*23 **Search me, O God, and know my heart;***
test me and know my anxious thoughts.
24 Point out anything in me that offends you,
and lead me along the path of everlasting life.

Psalm 46 tells us to stop striving and to know that God is God. The first verse refers to God as our refuge and strength. He is always ready to help us in times of trouble.

Psalm 46:10 NLT

Be still, and know that I am God.

Psalm 46:10 NASB1995

Cease striving and know that I am God.

> Sometimes, God allows us to get into places of striving so our faith will grow, and we acknowledge Him as our refuge and strength.

The verb "Be still" literally means "Take your hands off! Relax!". Many read this verse as a gentle reminder or an invitation to fellowship with God. But it is a rebuke to the nations coming against God's people and the Hebrews for their lack of trust. Sometimes, God allows us to get into places of striving so our faith will grow, and we acknowledge Him as our refuge, strength, and help as the Psalm begins. God's Word always presents a way out and instructions to help. We must go to Scripture and trust that the Spirit will teach and equip us.

Satan will pull out all the stops to keep us striving. Our mind is his battlefield. His tactics distract us from the truth of God's Word and our calling to walk in obedience. I call his tactics of distraction - *distractics*. They are meant to deceive us, cause us to doubt, and destroy anything good in our lives. Satan's only mission is to oppose the things of God. We can wisely learn to notice the uneasiness and trust that God has alerted our Spirit to a heart issue that needs to be addressed.

God's Word equips us to fight against the distractics of the evil one and stand firm in our faith. John writes to the children of God, the mature and the young in the faith.

1 John 2:14

God's word lives in your hearts,
and you have won your battle with the evil one.

Below are three steps I have identified to help me move out of the destructive patterns of striving. I have found that I can strive toward good things that keep me from God's best, which can also be destructive. I am super independent. When I feel threatened, overwhelmed, or not valued, my attitude instantly flips to dependence on myself. That is part of my fight, flight, fawn, or freeze coping mechanism. I fight by taking matters into my own hands and will move toward self-protection. God has healed relationships and my heart by making me very sensitive to what is going on in my mind and body. He has given me a strong sense of knowing when I am striving. I trust God to bring awareness and turn me toward His Word. I trust God will do this for you as you faithfully walk with Him and grow in Godliness.

Awareness

First, we need to be aware of our striving. Pray asking God for guidance and to show you where you are struggling. He will lovingly guide you. Below are questions to help narrow down a few areas God wants to address.

- What relationships are difficult or complicated? What is the role you play in this relationship?

- Do you struggle with people-pleasing?

- What circumstances are challenging right now? What expectations do you have that are not being met?

- What is your current perspective on life? Are you having a rough time, or could you be lingering in fear, anxiety, and worry?

Do you find yourself in any of these toxic "C" behaviors? These are gigantic triggers for striving.

Comparison

Don't be too quick to say you don't have an issue in this area. If you scroll through a social media feed, it is almost a subconscious attack. What about your neighbors, siblings, and friends? Do you compare?

Galatians 1:10

Obviously, I'm not trying to win the approval of people, but of God. If pleasing people were my goal, I would not be Christ's servant.

Complaining or criticizing

It is still complaining even if you are justified or only joining in to complain about something everyone else is.

James 5:9

Don't grumble about each other, brothers and sisters, or you will be judged. For look—the Judge is standing at the door!

Commiserating

Have you ever been with friends venting about disrespectful kids, frustrating husbands, or crappy jobs, and it ends up a festival of negativity? Sometimes, you can have empathy, but you should back out when it moves to negativity. Try not to get trapped in validating poor behavior.

1 Corinthians 15:33

Don't be fooled by those who say such things,
for bad company corrupts good character.

Acknowledge

With God's help, we acknowledge our striving. Everything God wants to do in you and through your life is an exchange. You must be willing to let go of your lies, expectations, and needs and allow Him to show what He has for you. When you exchange your striving with God, He gives you peace, joy, and contentment.

You put off the old self, our old sinful nature of striving and self-reliance, and we put on the new self through grace and trust in God.

> ### What is God asking you to exchange?

What is God asking you to exchange?

Where is He calling you to surrender and trust Him to provide, protect, and give you peace?

I learned about this practice of put off and put on during my Biblical Counseling courses. Through prayer and reflection, God will give us awareness of our sins or striving, and then we can take our specific issues to His Word for instruction.

2 Timothy 3:15-17

You have been taught the holy Scriptures from childhood, and they have given you the wisdom to receive the salvation that comes by trusting in Christ Jesus. All Scripture is inspired by God and is useful to teach us what is true and to make us realize what is wrong in our lives. It corrects us when we are wrong and teaches us to do what is right. God uses it to prepare and equip his people to do every good work.

What does Scripture teach about put off and put on for those in Christ?

All the following put-off and put-on verses are from the English Standard Version.

Colossians 3:9

Do not lie to one another, seeing that you have put off the old self with its practices.

Ephesians 4:22

to put off your old self which belongs to your former manner of life and is corrupt through deceitful desires.

Romans 13:12

The night is far gone; the day is at hand. So then let us cast off the works of darkness and put on the armor of light.

Once we acknowledge the sin we must put off, we surrender our power to God to put on our new nature in Christ.

Colossians 3:10 ESV

and have put on the new self, which is being renewed in knowledge after the image of its creator.

Colossians 3:12-14 ESV

Put on then, as God's chosen ones, holy and beloved, compassionate hearts, kindness, humility, meekness, and patience, bearing with one another and, if one has a complaint against another, forgiving each other; as the Lord has forgiven you, so you also must forgive. And above all these put-on love, which binds everything together in perfect harmony.

Ephesians 4:24 ESV

and to put on the new self, created after the likeness of God in true righteousness and holiness.

Romans 13:12 ESV

The night is far gone; the day is at hand. So then let us cast off the works of darkness and put on the armor of light.

Romans 13:14 ESV

But put on the Lord Jesus Christ, and make no provision for the flesh, to gratify its desires.

Here is how I practically apply this exchange of put-off and put-on. In the first column of the chart below, I have listed a few striving issues I struggled with and became aware of with God's help. The middle two columns list insight from Scripture; the last column is what I put on instead through prayer and meditating on the Word of God.

Put off	Put off Scripture	Put on Scripture	Put on
Bitterness	Heb 12:15	Eph 4:32	Tenderhearted and forgiving
Selfishness	Phil 2:21	John 12:24	Self-Denial
Pride	Proverbs 16:5	James 4:6	Humility
Disobedience	1 Samuel 12:15	Deuteronomy 11:27	Obedience
Ungratefulness	Romans 1:21	Ephesians 5:20	Gratefulness
Anger	Proverbs 29:22	Galatians 5:22-23	Self-Control

A helpful expanded table of topics is available on my website if you would like to identify your problem areas. Consider applying WRAP to each verse to help you meditate and learn what God wants to teach you.

Act in Obedience

> The Bible is our roadmap for walking in obedience. Scripture will illuminate the path for us to walk and guide us as we navigate this world.

Lastly, we act in obedience. The Bible is our roadmap for walking in obedience. Scripture will illuminate the path for us to walk and guide us as we navigate this world. (Proverbs 6:23) Our daily walk is a lifestyle of seeking to know God by meditating on His Word. The Scripture below clearly shows that obedience is about loving God and surrendering. I can't make you obedient. I can make a case for obedience based on my own experience and what God's Word says, but ultimately, the condition of your heart will determine your obedience. Is it rooted in love through faith?

1 John 5:3

Loving God means keeping his commandments, and His commandments are not burdensome.

1 John 2:5

But those who obey God's word truly show how completely they love him. That is how we know we are living in him.

Luke 9:23

Then he said to the crowd, "If any of you wants to be my follower, you must give up your own way, take up your cross daily, and follow me."

What do you obey? Why? If we are like most people, we obey because we expect some reward, want to avoid a negative consequence, or genuinely believe in authority. Obedience to God's Word is no different. We may consider the reward for obedience to be eternal life in Heaven, or we obey to escape the negative consequence of hell. Maybe both are true. I believe these are benefits of our obedience, but our true obedience comes from our faith and love. Faithful obedience is done because we love God and believe in His way, and the authority found in His Word is the Truth.

Consider this observation from Henri Nouwen.

"The obedient life develops our abilities to hear and sense God's presence and activities. The word

> The obedient life develops our abilities to hear and sense God's presence and activities.

obedience includes the word *audire*, which means "listening." The obedient life is one in which we listen with great attention to God's Spirit within and among us. The great news of God's revelation is not simply that God exists, but also that God is actively present. Our God is a God who cares, heals, guides, directs, challenges, confronts, corrects, and forms us. God is a God who wants to lead us closer to the full realization of our lionhearted humanity, if you will. To be obedient means to be constantly attentive to this active presence and to allow God, who is only love, to be the source as well as the goal of all we think, say, and do."[19]

I want a faith that is constantly attentive to God's presence so that all I think, say, and do reflect Him. In the next chapter, we examine what Scripture says about this posture of attentiveness and how we can do it. It's another "A" word: Abide.

WRAP Yourself in the Word

Write

Write the Word

Which passage will you write? Pick one from this chapter to remind your heart of God's goodness, love, or provision. I am choosing the passages we looked at in Colossians.

---

19 Nouwen, H. J. M. (2018). *Spiritual Direction*. HarperCollins.

Colossians 3:9-10 ESV

"Do not lie to one another, seeing that you have put off the old self with its practices and have put on the new self, which is being renewed in knowledge after the image of its creator."

Colossians 3:9-10 NLT

"Don't lie to each other, for you have stripped off your old sinful nature and all its wicked deeds. Put on your new nature and be renewed as you learn to know your Creator and become like him."

Read

Read the Word

1. Read it to yourself.

2. Read it out loud to yourself.

3. Read it to someone else.

Ask/Apply

Apply the Word

- List the promises, instructions, or commands in this passage.

- What is the most important thing God wants me to see in this passage?

- Is there any unconfessed sin I need to talk to God about?

- Where do I need God's help responding to this passage?

Pray

Pray the Word.

Father, renew me in the knowledge of your love. Remind me that I am created in your image and becoming like you as I leave behind my old self and the sinful practices that used to define me. Give me the wisdom to choose daily to put on my new nature found in Jesus. I love and choose to obey you. When my flesh is weak, you make me strong. I love you, Jesus, and rejoice that I am a new creature who can surrender all my striving to You. AMEN.

Growth Challenge

Reread this chapter and ask God to help you listen to His Spirit with great attention.

Chapter Twelve

Abide in the Vine

It is the Holy Spirit who encourages and enables us to abide.
He teaches us the Word; He enables us to pray;
He reveals our sins; He gives us the inward desire to obey God.

Warren Wiersbe

My favorite Gospel is John because John wrote it for all people, focused on the teachings of Jesus and His deity, and in the verse below shared his purpose for writing the book.

John 30-31

The disciples saw Jesus do many other miraculous signs in addition to the ones recorded in this book. But these are written so that you may continue to believe that Jesus is the Messiah, the Son of God and that by believing in him you will have life by the power of his name.

It is written so we may believe and have life. One of the ways John illustrates this life, our relationship with Jesus, is found in John 15 when he compares our relationship to that of a vine and branch. Our life is found attached to the vine, Jesus. Our daily nourishment comes from the connection we have to the vine. If we were ever cut off from the vine, we would die. John calls this abiding. John begins the chapter with the final and seventh "I AM" statements of Jesus.

John 15:1 ESV

"I am the true vine, and my Father is the vinedresser."

In chapters 13 through 17, John captures Jesus preparing the disciples for what will come. It begins in chapter 13 when He washes their feet and predicts how He will be betrayed. In chapter 14, Jesus promises the Holy Spirit.

John 14:15-16

"If you love me, obey my commandments. And I will ask the Father, and he will give you another Advocate, who will never leave you."

Jesus also tells them that the Holy Spirit, His representative, will teach them everything and remind them of everything that Jesus had told them. In chapter 16, Jesus warns the followers that the world will hate them but never fall away, no matter how bad it gets. They are to continue spreading the message of the Gospel. In chapter 17, we find Jesus praying for himself, the disciples, and us.

Chapter 15 focuses on where we find the command to abide. Note that the NLT uses the word *remain* instead of *abiding*, but it is the same Greek word *meno*, meaning to be kept or remain.

John 15:1-5

"I am the true grapevine, and my Father is the gardener. He cuts off every branch of mine that doesn't produce fruit, and he prunes the branches that do bear fruit so they will produce even more. You have already been pruned and purified by the message I have given you. Remain in me, and I will remain in you. For a branch cannot produce fruit if it is severed from the vine, and you cannot be fruitful unless you remain in me. Yes, I am the vine; you are the branches. Those who remain in me, and I in them, will produce much fruit. For apart from me, you can do nothing."

Note the facts found in the above passage:

- Jesus is the Vine.
- God is the Gardener, Vinedresser.
- God prunes the branches.
- We are the branches.
- We abide in Jesus – He abides in us.
- When we abide, we produce fruit.
- Without abiding in Jesus, we don't produce fruit.
- Apart from Jesus, we can do nothing.

John 15:6-8

"Anyone who does not remain in me is thrown away like a useless branch and withers. Such branches are gathered into a pile to be burned. But if you remain in me and my words remain in you, you may ask for anything you want, and it will be granted! When you produce much fruit, you are my true disciples. This brings great glory to my Father."

Fruit is evidence of a true disciple. We produce much fruit when we abide.

Jesus is comparing two types of branches in these verses: Believers and unbelievers.

- When there is no abiding – the branch is thrown away and withers – burned.
- When we abide in Jesus – our prayers are answered.
- Fruit is evidence of a true disciple. We produce much fruit when we abide.
- God is glorified when we abide.

John 15:9

"I have loved you even as the Father has loved me. Remain in my love. When you obey my commandments, you remain in my love, just as I obey my Father's commandments and remain in his love. I have told you these things so that you will be filled with my joy. Yes, your joy will overflow!"

- Jesus loves as the Father loves Him.
- We abide because we love.
- Abiding enables obedience. Just as Jesus was obedient to God.
- Abiding produces joy overflowing.

John 15:12-17

"This is my commandment: Love each other in the same way I have loved you. There is no greater love than to lay down one's life for one's friends. You are my friends if you do what I command. I no longer call you slaves, because a master doesn't confide in his slaves. Now you are my friends, since I have told you everything the Father told me. You didn't choose me. I chose you. I appointed you to go and produce lasting fruit, so that the Father will give you whatever you ask for, using my name. This is my command: Love each other."

The commands:

- Love others the way Jesus loves us.
- This great love is reserved for friends, not from obligation as slaves.
- We are Jesus's friends, and He shares what God has told Him
- Jesus chose us.
- Jesus appoints us to produce fruit.
- Father answers prayers.

The Fruit of Abiding

> As disciples, we bear fruit because God never gives up on us.

God is shaping you into the person He designed you to be, and the pruning in this process is complicated and painful. As disciples, we bear fruit because God never gives up on us. This abiding is a connection of life. The very sap of the vine flows through us when we are connected and abiding. It isn't an emotion or feeling but a fixed position. It doesn't come upon us in Church on Sunday during worship and leave when we encounter difficulty or resistance at work, home, or the grocery store. We are united with Christ through faith; we can do nothing apart from Him. One commentary puts it this way. "Oh, we can sing in the choir, give an offering, answer questions at small group, hand out bulletins, or go Christmas caroling, but apart from him, those things are in our strength and therefore are not pleasing to God. They are the "fruit" of our own effort, the "fruit" of self-righteousness."

The fruit produced from an ongoing surrender of ourselves to abiding in Jesus over everything is both for our benefit and for others. We have talked about abiding throughout this book.

- The tree in Psalm 1 is a picture of abiding.
- The practice of WRAP is a practice of abiding.

- Sit, walk, stand is an illustration of abiding.

- Surrender striving is an act of obedience and abiding.

- Our faith is evidence of abiding.

Now, where do you see fruit in your life?

Where can you draw closer to God? Not sure?

Ask God to examine your heart and trust Him to guide you. Prayer is our connection to abiding. Through prayer,

> Prayer is our connection to abiding.

we not only make requests to God, but through His Spirit, we can listen and hear God's voice. We can discern, grow in wisdom, and worship Him. Your answered prayers depend on how you abide.

Answered Prayer is a Fruit of Abiding

We know prayer is our communication with Jesus, and it strengthens our faith and relationship with Him. God listens to our prayers when we engage with the Word and respond in prayer. Our prayers are answered when we abide with Jesus.

Here is an illustration of an abiding prayer relationship with God.

- We receive the Word that informs, instructs, and commands.

- We respond in Prayer shaped by the Word.

- God hears our prayers and responds by shaping our desires through the Holy Spirit.
- We respond in prayer according to the Word.
- God answers according to the Word.

> **Does Scripture shape your prayer?**

Does Scripture shape your prayer?

Is it an overflow from the life flowing in you because you are connected to the Vine?

Obedient Love is a Fruit of Abiding

God loves Jesus, Jesus loves us, and we respond to this love through obedience.

> **Our obedience doesn't earn God's love; it is evidence of our love for God.**

Our obedience doesn't earn God's love; it is evidence of our love for God.

Jesus's love in us will produce the fruit of obedience when we abide. His life in you will cause you to love what He loves, treasure His Word, and obey out of joy, not obligation. You will delight in His law as you meditate on it, and He will shape your heart to be like His. This is another way to picture the sanctification process.

1 John 4:15-16 (ESV)

Whoever confesses that Jesus is the Son of God, God abides in him, and he in God. So, we have come to know and to believe the love that God has for us. God is love, and whoever abides in love abides in God, and God abides in him.

When we abide in love, we are equipped to share the Gospel and love others. This love is not as the world loves. Our love is part of our nature as born-again Christians. John expands on love and abiding in his letter to Christians in 1 John.

1 John 4:7-8

Dear friends, let us continue to love one another, for love comes from God. Anyone who loves is a child of God and knows God. But anyone who does not love does not know God, for God is love.

John is talking about knowing God. Because God is love and we are created in His image, we know Him and have this love in us. In the Bible, the word know has a deeper meaning than simply acquiring facts or having an intellectual understanding. To know God means we have a deep, intimate relationship with Him. We share His life and enjoy His love. We know His truth.

1 John 2:3-5

And we can be sure that we know him if we obey his commandments. If someone claims, "I know God," but doesn't obey God's commandments, that person is a liar and is not living in the truth. But those who obey God's word truly show how completely they love him. That is how we know we are living in him.

Inexhaustible Joy is the Fruit of Abiding

> Joy is evidence that we are genuine disciples of Jesus.

Joy is evidence that we are genuine disciples of Jesus.

One commentary on John puts it this way. "Joy in Jesus is inseparable from knowing and following him. You can't know him and lack joy. You can't follow him and lack joy. You can't be united with him and lack joy. It's a biblical, logical, and theological impossibility. It does not mean every day is easy and filled with laughter, but it does mean your life is ultimately marked by a confidence that Jesus is greater and more satisfying than anything this world has to offer."[20]

Our joy in Christ is not related to the circumstances of our lives but to our unchanging relationship with God.

---

20 Carter, M., & Wredberg, J. (2017). *Exalting Jesus in John.* B&H Publishing Group.

Psalm 16:11

You will show me the way of life, granting me the joy of your presence and the pleasures of living with you forever.

When you received the Holy Spirit, you received the Godly attitude of the fruits of the Spirit.

Galatians 5:22

But the Holy Spirit produces this kind of fruit in our lives: love, joy, peace, patience, kindness, goodness, faithfulness, gentleness, and self-control. There is no law against these things.

Joy is an experience of knowing that all is well between us and God. Even when trials come and our life circumstances are difficult, we can have joy. It is a gift from God.

> Even when trials come and our life circumstances are difficult, we can have joy. It is a gift from God.

Sacrificial Love is Fruit of Abiding

Jesus commands us to love others as He has loved us. How is that possible? That is a perfect standard. He says that the act of friendship and love is to lay down our life for a friend. He wants us to see that the greatest love isn't romantic or erotic but sacrificial. Jesus makes this love a defining characteristic of being His follower. Without love, it is impossible to be connected to the Vine. Apart from Him, we can do nothing. But God has provided a helper, called the Advocate. (John 14:16) The Holy Spirit testifies to everything Jesus teaches.

If Jesus lives in us, we will be different. We act, live, and love differently. This difference isn't because of our strength. It is because we live a surrendered life to the work of Jesus in us. Understanding the power of abiding by our identity in Christ is foundational to our Christian life.

As we grow in this understanding of abiding in Christ, we will grow in Godliness and bear more fruit. This fruit is evidence of our faith. Our self-centered striving will not produce lasting fruit, but our abiding fruit has seed to produce more fruit, so we continue to produce fruit.

Luke 8:15

And the seeds that fell on the good soil represent honest, good-hearted people who hear God's word, cling to it, and patiently produce a huge harvest.

Abiding in the vine produces the fruit of righteousness. In his second letter to the believers dispersed through Asia Minor, modern-day Turkey, Peter tells us that from the power of knowing or placing our faith in Christ, God has given us everything we need to live a godly life. The promises of abundant and eternal life are ours because of our faith in Christ.

2 Peter 1:3-4

By his divine power, God has given us everything we need for living a godly life. We have received all of this by coming to know him, the one who called us to himself by means of his marvelous glory and excellence. And because of his glory and excellence, he has given us great and precious promises. These are the promises that enable you to share his divine nature and escape the world's corruption caused by human desires.

As God's children, we share His nature through the Holy Spirit and escape the power of corruption caused by human desires. That doesn't mean we won't experience sinful human desires, but we have the power to overcome corruption. We have the power to overcome the evilness that exists in our thoughts, emotions, and will.

Because of the faith we have placed in the person of Jesus, we experience God's power, His glory, and excellence. Peter proclaims that through the sufficiency of Scripture, we have everything we need to live a Godly life. We have the nature of God through the Holy Spirit living in us.

> ## Our spiritual growth is not automatic. It requires us to participate.

Through Scripture, the Holy Spirit teaches us how to grow in Godliness and escape the sinful lifestyle.

Our spiritual growth is not automatic. It requires us to participate, and Peter tells us what to do in the following verses. The eight qualities that follow are a map that shows us how to progress in our sanctification or Christian maturity. We move progressively toward Godliness as we practice these eight qualities.

2 Peter 1:5-9

In view of all this, make every effort to respond to God's promises. Supplement your faith with a generous provision of moral excellence (virtue), *and moral excellence with knowledge, and knowledge with self-control, and self-control with patient endurance* (perseverance), *and patient endurance with godliness, and godliness with brotherly affection, and brotherly affection with love for everyone.*

True disciples bear fruit because God's power is alive and actively working in them. As we progressively practice these qualities, we produce good fruit. Hear what Peter goes on to promise.

> True disciples bear fruit because God's power is alive and actively working in them.

2 Peter 1:10

So, dear brothers and sisters, work hard to prove that you really are among those God has called and chosen. Do these things, and you will never fall away.

Our fruitfulness will be evidence of our faith, our abiding. Our lives will show the fruit of our abiding. We will be like the tree planted by streams of water that bears fruit in season, whose leaves never wither, and whatever we do in Jesus' name will always prosper. (Psalm 1:3)

WRAP Yourself in the Word

Write

Write the Word

Write out the following verse:

John 15:5

"Yes, I am the vine; you are the branches. Those who remain in me, and I in them, will produce much fruit. For apart from me, you can do nothing."

John 15:16-17

"You didn't choose me. I chose you. I appointed you to go and produce lasting fruit, so that the Father will give you whatever you ask for, using my name. This is my command: Love each other."

Read

Read the Word

1. Read it to yourself.

2. Read it out loud to yourself.

3. Read it to someone else.

Ask/Apply

Apply the Word

- List the promises, instructions, or commands in this passage.

- What is the most important thing God wants me to see in this passage?

- Is there any unconfessed sin I need to talk to God about?

- Where do I need God's help responding to this passage?

Pray

Pray the Word

Father, never let me go. I want to abide in you all of the days of my life. Your ways are freedom from my striving. I want to experience the joy found in abiding in you. I know life will be hard and have trials and sorrow, but I will always have the joy of my salvation. I welcome all that you have for me. I rejoice that I can come to you daily, and my prayer will be heard. I am not alone. With the Holy Spirit at work in me, help me love others as you love me. Let my love glorify you as I seek to abide in you with every breath. AMEN.

Growth Challenge

Where do you find joy? Make a list. For three days, list ten joys in your life each day. If you find a lack of joy in your life, you should examine your habits of abiding.

Chapter Thirteen

Invitation to Grow in Godliness

All Scripture is inspired by God and is useful to teach us what is true and to make us realize what is wrong in our lives. It corrects us when we are wrong and teaches us to do what is right. God uses it to prepare and equip his people to do every good work.

2 Timothy 3:16-17

WRAP Yourself in the Word was God's invitation for me to understand my value to Him and recognize my identity in Christ. The intimate time I spent writing His Word was a response I offered to God's gentle call to a deeper relationship. The more I learned of God's ways, the more I understood my purpose. This was a personal journey. Looking back, I see God's faithfulness so clearly. The many ways He used my circumstances, personality,

> The more I learned of God's ways, the more I understood my purpose.

unique interests, deeply held beliefs, and the specific people He placed in my life, from the tree analogy in Psalm 1 to the sliver of hope when I cried out to Him for help.

I remember a thought inventory I did early in my healing journey. The thoughts I set out to notice were only those I told myself repeatedly. I logged the thoughts I began to say out loud that I previously only said to myself. One thought I believed and often said out loud was, "I know God's promises are real, but I don't believe they are true for me." I noticed that I only began to voice these thoughts when God placed me in situations with people I trusted. I slowly began to share some of my darkest thoughts with other people. The most beautiful part of sharing these thoughts was finding out I was not alone. People I trusted and loved could relate, and they encouraged me. They also helped me see the faulty thinking in my thoughts and beliefs. Isolation is another distractic from Satan. He will keep us trapped, believing a lie that we are alone and the only one who suffers from a particular thought or issue. We believe what we tell ourselves, even if it's a lie. This works in darkness and for good, but the point is our thoughts are powerful. I had believed the lies for so long, but when I began to share and bring the lies into the light, the power of the lies began to fade.

Scripture has something to say about this theme of light and darkness. The following passages teach us that Jesus is light; if Jesus lives in us, we do not live in darkness. Satan's lies will never extinguish the light that lives in us.

John 1:4-5

The Word gave life to everything that was created, and his life brought light to everyone. The light shines in the darkness, and the darkness can never extinguish it.

John 8:12

Jesus spoke to the people once more and said, "I am the light of the world. If you follow me, you won't have to walk in darkness because you will have the light that leads to life.

John 12:46

I have come as a light to shine in this dark world so that all who put their trust in me will no longer remain in the dark.

Claiming these promises over our lives clears up faulty self-talk and generates healing in our hearts. We replace the old message, the lie, with the new message, the truth found in Scripture. (See Chapter 2 Write)

The journey through the WRAP practice was also an invitation to get to know myself, what I believed about God, and how that impacted

> Claiming these promises over our lives clears up faulty self-talk and generates healing in our hearts.

my view of self. For example, the faulty belief about God's promises not being true for me represented that I thought I was an exception to God's Word. I believed in my darkness that God would exclude me from all the promises. That lie and belief limited God's power in my life. My focus was on me and my inadequacies – a Joni-centered life. What we believe about God, His goodness, His Word, His power, and His presence impacts everything.

Applying the practical truth of God's Word to our lives will continually meet obstacles if our understanding of God is skewed. We wrongly view God through the lens of our perspective rather than see ourselves through the truth of who God is. A. W. Tozer once said, "The most important thing about a person is what comes to mind when they think about God."[21] We live – rightly or wrongly – out of our belief in the existence and character of God. Our view of God shapes our identity, influences our purpose, and impacts our value. Consider the following questions:

> We wrongly view God through the lens of our perspective rather than see ourselves through the truth of who God is.

- What comes to mind when you think of God?

- What comes to mind when you think about yourself?

21 Tozer, A. W. (2022). *The Knowledge of the Holy: The Attributes of God. Their Meaning in the Christian Life.* Lutterworth Press.

- What do you think comes to God's mind when He thinks about you?

WRAP Yourself in the Word was a personal inward journey that led to my greatest healing. It was also an invitation to be in community with Jesus and others. I left my Joni-centered life, saw how God works in others, and designed me to be in community with others. The invitation was for me to understand my value, identity, and purpose. I needed to understand and embrace that Jesus has viewed me as a VIP (very important person) since birth. I've always been a VIP, but I couldn't see, hear, or know until I began to spend time with Him. WRAP Yourself in the Word was an invitation to see myself in His Word. We must spend time with God in His Word to know what He says about us – that we are VIPs.

Invitation to WRAP Yourself in the Word

WRAP Yourself in the Word is now an invitation I make to you.

Do you believe you are a VIP?

Do you know your Value to God?

Do you abide in and walk in your Identity in Christ?

Do you understand your Purpose?

Living as a VIP in Christ is how God created us to live. We were not made for the world we live in now. We were created for more. WRAP Yourself in the Word is a simple practice that led to my greatest healing. It led me to live a

VIP life. If you have trouble believing you are a VIP, I'd love to help.

Together, I will help you learn to sit, walk, and stand in who God created you to be. I will help you learn to desire God's Word and delight in it day and night. I will help you take the truths in God's Word and speak them to your heart until you sense God is near. I will help you build your confidence in His Word so you can shift your focus from yourself to what God wants to do in and through you. You will build a confident faith that perseveres, surrenders and abides. I will help you do your part, and together, we will ask for God's guidance and seek His faithfulness. He will reveal Himself to you, and you will begin to know the God who loves you.

> When you know how much God loves you and the Value you hold and let that fully rest in your heart, it becomes the lens through which you see every part of your life.

When you know how much God loves you and the Value you hold and let that fully rest in your heart, it becomes the lens through which you see every part of your life. You begin to understand the magnitude of the Christ's sacrifice. The Biblical lens changes how you see yourself and your Identity in Christ. When we put our complete confidence in who we are in Christ, the

Holy Spirit enables us to live out the Purpose that God designed for us from the beginning. We develop a confident faith that believes God is who He said He is and will do what He said He would do. We trust that God has a more excellent plan for us, and we begin to walk in obedience because of our love for Him.

When you embrace the freedom and grace in understanding your Value, Identity, and Purpose as a child of God, you can trust God to shape your character as you grow in Virtue. Knowing that it is God's will for you to be progressively transformed into His image, you surrender your hearts to abide in Jesus. Growing and abiding in Christ produces the fruit that is evidence of our faith, which will spill out of your life with Influence on your family and community. How God uses this influence will be a rewarding journey of discovery and continued surrender. God will begin to shape you into a vessel that resembles who He created you to be from birth. He will continue to invite you into a deeper relationship and ask you to align your Priorities with His purpose and plan for you. Believing you are a

> God will begin to shape you into a vessel that resembles who He created you to be from birth. He will continue to invite you into a deeper relationship and ask you to align your Priorities with His purpose and plan for you.

VIP in Christ transforms your heart, and you will live like a VIP in Christ.

This is a model for discipleship. It is the model God used in my life to teach me through His Word. He carried me through darkness into the light. I believe He wants to do through me that which He has done and continues to do in me. He invited me to use what I have learned to help others live out a Full-Time Faith and to experience being deeply loved as a treasured child of God.

The VIP experience is a discipleship model that combines teaching, coaching, and mentoring. I work with individuals, groups, and Christian teams in the workplace. This is accomplished over several weeks in a flexible meeting format. I bring additional resources into the experience, including books, training, and Bible studies that all impacted my most significant healing and continue to support and encourage growth.

Remember, I am on the same path of becoming like Jesus. Maybe I am a few steps further down the path, but I have not reached perfection. God has uniquely used my past, my talents and skills, and my specific suffering to be in a position to teach, coach, and mentor others. I seek His guidance and help the same way I teach you. Below is a brief outline and directing questions of the VIP framework we work through in two rounds.

VIP: Establish the Foundation

- Value – What does God value? What does He say about our value? What do I value? Does it line up with what God values?

- Identity – Who do I say God is? Who does He say I am? Who do I believe I am? How do I balance my Identity with all the roles and responsibilities God has given me?

- Purpose – What is God's purpose? What does He say about my purpose? What do I believe is my purpose? How do I reflect God's purpose?

VIP: Building a Faith

- Virtues – Character – What does God say about my character and how to grow Godly virtues? What is the current state of my character? How does what I value or how I see my value impact my character growth?

- Influence – What is my influence? How do I use my influence? Where can I use it to fulfill my purpose? How does my identity or what I believe about my identity impact my influence?

- Priorities – What are my priorities? How do my thoughts, talents, time, and treasures indicate my priorities? Do I need to adjust my priorities to align with my purpose?

The goals of the VIP framework:

1. Living in your God-given Value defines how you grow in Virtue.

> The confidence you have in your Identity in Christ determines your Influence.

2. The confidence you have in your Identity in Christ determines your Influence.

3. Knowing your created Purpose directs your priorities.

I mentioned that I use teaching, mentoring, and coaching methods. Here is how I see these roles used in the VIP framework.

Teaching: As a teacher, I will facilitate learning new concepts or encourage you to view something differently. I will help you understand how you learn so that you can encounter it differently as you grow in your faith and understanding of God's Word.

Mentor: As a mentor, I will remind you of what you know and what you have learned and offer advice based on my experience with God's Word. I will answer questions and direct you to additional resources to provide more information. I am a guide for you and will help you on your journey.

Coach: As a coach, I will ask open-ended and probing questions that will require you to do some self-discovery. I will help you navigate false beliefs and feelings. Coaching is always focused on the future, your wants, and the changes you hope to achieve.

Life coaching has become a popular industry. You can hire a life coach to help you in every aspect of your life. I have hired a coach for different challenges in my life. My book coach was a gift as I struggled to put together the structure and content. She was encouraging and helped me stay on track with deadlines. I take my role as a faith coach or discipleship coach seriously. I will walk with you and encourage you as you grow in your faith. I also encourage you to live in community with others as you go through the VIP framework. We were not created to live in isolation and do life on our own – remember that is a distractic from Satan.

And, of course, a foundational part of the VIP framework is our WRAP Yourself in the Word practice. We even expand on the WRAP practice and learn more ways to study the Bible, deepening your application of God's Word. You will learn more about the transforming power of prayer.

A Final WRAP Yourself in the Word

We are living in a time that requires believers to be alert and ready to answer the hope we have in Jesus. The Apostle Paul puts it this way.

1 Peter 1:13-16

So prepare your minds for action and exercise self-control. Put all your hope in the gracious salvation that will come to you when Jesus Christ is revealed to the world. So, you must live as God's obedient children. Don't slip back into your old ways of living to satisfy your desires. You didn't know any better then. But now you must be holy in everything you do, just as God who chose you is holy. The Scriptures say, "You must be holy because I am holy."

We are instructed to ask for wisdom, and from this wisdom, we must put our hope in God alone so we can stand in times of darkness now and for what is coming. James, the brother of Jesus, offers us this advice.

James 1:5-7

If you need wisdom, ask our generous God, and he will give it to you. He will not rebuke you for asking. But when you ask him, be sure that your faith is in God alone. Do not waver, for a person with divided loyalty is as unsettled as a wave of the sea that is blown and tossed by the wind.

228

I sincerely desire that you are inspired to seek a deeper relationship with our Holy God. I believe our salvation is secure once we accept Jesus, but God wants much more for us in this life. Our eternity is now; it doesn't start when we die. We exist in eternity. Our location in eternity changes when we die. We live in the tension that we *already* possess all that we need to lead a Godly life but are *not yet* like Jesus. Our citizenship is *already* in heaven, but we do *not yet* reside there. We are *already* spiritually resurrected but *not yet* physically resurrected. Trusting in both the *already* and the *not-yet* requires faith. I hope you will live with trust, joy, endurance, and worship as you live in this tension of the *already* and *not yet*.

Peter talks about our inheritance in heaven and how God protects us through faith until the last day.

> Our eternity is now; it doesn't start when we die. We exist in eternity. Our location in eternity changes when we die.
>
> Our citizenship is already in heaven, but we do not yet reside there.

1 Peter 1:6-8

So be truly glad. There is wonderful joy ahead, even though you must endure many trials for a little while. These trials will show that your faith is genuine. It is being tested as fire tests and purifies gold—though your faith is far more precious than mere gold. So, when your faith remains strong through many trials, it will bring you much praise and glory and honor on the day when Jesus Christ is revealed to the whole world. You love him even though you have never seen him. Though you do not see him now, you trust him, and you rejoice with a glorious, inexpressible joy.

Will you live a Full-Time Faith full of love, trust, and inexpressible joy with me in the tension of the *already* and *not yet* praising God with all honor and glory?

Lastly, I pray for you again this prayer from Paul.

Ephesians 3:14-21

"When I think of all this, I fall to my knees and pray to the Father, the Creator of everything in heaven and on earth. I pray that from his glorious, unlimited resources, he will empower you with inner strength through his Spirit. Then Christ will make his home in your hearts as you trust in him. Your roots will grow down into God's love and keep you strong. And may you have the power to understand, as all God's people should, how wide, how long, how high, and how deep his love is. May you experience the love of Christ, though it is too great to understand fully. Then, you will be made complete with all the fullness of life and power that comes from God. Now, all glory to God, who is able, through his mighty power at work within us, to accomplish infinitely more than we might ask or think. Glory to him in the church and in Christ Jesus through all generations, forever and ever! Amen.

WRAP Yourself in the Word

Write

Write the Word

Write the following verse:

1 Peter 1:6-8:

"So be truly glad. There is wonderful joy ahead, even though you must endure many trials for a little while. These trials will show that your faith is genuine. It is being tested as fire tests and purifies gold—though your faith is far more precious than mere gold. So, when your faith remains strong through many trials, it will bring you much praise and glory and honor on the day when Jesus Christ is revealed to the whole world. You love him even though you have never seen him. Though you do not see him now, you trust him, and you rejoice with a glorious, inexpressible joy."

Read

Read the Word

1. Read it to yourself.
2. Read it out loud to yourself.
3. Read it to someone else.
4. Read it again while smiling.

Apply

Apply the Word

- List the promises, instructions, or commands in this passage.

- What is the most important thing God wants me to see in this passage?

- Is there any unconfessed sin I need to talk to God about?

- Where do I need God's help responding to this passage?

Pray

Pray the Word

Father, help us understand the wonderful joy that is ahead for us. Help us keep our eyes fixed on your promises as we endure trials. Remind us that our testing is refining us and purifying us like gold. We are precious to you. Although our trials feel like we have been forgotten, you are using them to strengthen our faith. Help us see your faithfulness in every trial. Father, we wait with joy and grateful hearts for the day Jesus is revealed to the whole world. We love Him. We trust Him. We rejoice with a glorious, inexpressible joy. Let the whole world see this joy so they are drawn to and desire your eternal salvation. AMEN.

Growth Challenge

Pray Ephesians 3:14-21 for yourself.

Father, When I think of all you have provided, I fall to my knees and pray. You are Father, the Creator of everything in heaven and on earth. I pray from your glorious, unlimited resources that you will empower me with inner strength through the Spirit. I invite Christ to make his home in my heart as I trust in Him. Cause my roots to grow down into your love and keep me strong. God grant me the power to understand, as all God's people should, how wide, how long, how high, and how deep your love is. I want to experience the love of Christ, though it is too great to understand fully. I want to be made complete with all the fullness of life and power that comes from you. Now all glory to you God, who is able, through your mighty power at work within us, accomplish infinitely more than I might ask or think. Glory to you and Christ Jesus through all generations, forever and ever! Amen

Acknowledgments

Every cheerleader needs a cheerleader. I am blessed to have an entire squad of cheerleaders. While this book has been many years in the making, God has been faithfully providing support along the way. Often, people jumped into the dark pit, sat with me, or stood on the bank and offered me a hand to grab and help pull me out. Many days, God sent encouragement with opportunities to serve others. I am grateful for the opportunity in this book to express some gratitude to the many people who have been my cheerleaders.

My husband and I attended different universities, and most of his friends only knew me as the cheerleader. They knew he was committed to a girl he knew in high school and was a cheerleader at a nearby university. To this day, many of them still refer to me as "the cheerleader." The ironic piece to that story is that my husband has been the biggest cheerleader in my life. He stood on the sidelines, not knowing how to help but always fighting for me. He never gave up, even when he had good reason to turn away. He was the voice of reason even when I disliked hearing it. He supported my healing journey just as fiercely. My healing brought healing to our hearts individually and our marriage. What a blessing God has given me in this man. He is the man I always hoped would love and cheer for me every day.

My children are also front-row members of the cheerleading squad. I see the very best of me in them. They also have some not-so-great parts of me, too. Sorry kids. They are perfect reflections of God's love and grace. They have journeyed through the rough spaces and now stand on the other side with me – celebrating the joy that has returned to our family. Thank you, kids, for never giving up and always needing your mom – you give me courage and hope and fill my life with joy.

God has blessed my life with incredible friendships, but two specifically have spoken through their megaphones to encourage me throughout writing this book. Before the book was an idea, my friend and spiritual mentor, Amanda, spent many hours listening, guiding me toward Scripture, and encouraging me to seek God's face, not my feelings. What a privilege to have begun our eternal friendship on this side of heaven.

In the home stretch of the book, God reconciled my heart to a dear friend with whom I have shared a lot of life. Amy, your coaching, curious questions about the book, and my progress in writing have been a true blessing. Thank you for reminding me what I know but don't always see in myself. Thank you for being part of my cheerleading team and co-fun-finder.

One unexpected relationship God used to confirm in my heart that this book was needed in the world was my sister-in-law, Annette. Caring for Annette during her last days on this earth was devastatingly hard and an extreme honor. She was curious about the book, why I was writing it, and how I would use it to share with others. God allowed me to share my journey with her and discover we had much in common. We could relate to each other's hurt and pain, yet our stories differed. She came to know Jesus when she lived with us, and I look forward to telling her about all the ways God used the book and hearing about the days she has spent with Jesus. Until then, Annette, thank you for cheering me on and trusting me with your heart.

Lastly, Mom. You were my first cheerleader. You haven't always been credited for the prayers, devotion, sacrifices, and support you've given. But I see you, the kind and giving person you are. Some would say you give too much and do too much for others at the expense of yourself. Caring for others is not easy, and you do it gracefully. Thank you for teaching me how to care for and love others. You are investing in eternal things just as we are called to do. I pray this book will be my way to also invest in eternal things. Love you.

Scripture References by Chapter

Chapter 1

Proverbs 3:5
Ephesians 3:14-21

Chapter 2

Philippians 4:8
2 Corinthians 10:5
Romans 12:1-2
Psalm 119:11
Psalm 1:2
Joshua   1:8
Exodus 17:14
Jeremiah 30:2
WRAP - Proverbs 3:5-6

Chapter 3

Exodus 20:3
Nehemiah 9:3, 8:8
1 Timothy 4:13
WRAP - Revelations 1:3

Chapter 4

Matthew 11:28-30
Psalm 1:3
Psalm 1:2
Psalm 1:1
WRAP – Matthew 11:28-30

Chapter 5

Matthew 6:9-13
Romans 8:26
Psalm 18:6
Psalm 34:17-18
Psalm 139:23-24
Psalm 3:11-12
Hebrew 12:10-11
Hebrew 4:12
John 17:17
2 Timothy 3:16-17
WRAP – Psalm 34:17-18

Chapter 6

Romans 3:23
Romans 6:23
Romans 5:8
Romans 10:9-10
Romans 10:13
Psalm 100:5
Numbers 23:19
Psalm 119:86
Deuteronomy 31:8

Jeremiah 29:12-14
Proverbs 3:5-6
Hebrews 11:1
2 Corinthians 5:7
1 Corinthians 2: 4-5
Isaiah 7:9
Isaiah 55:8-9
John 15:5
Galatians 2:20
Isaiah 41:10
Isaiah 46:9-11
John 15:14-17, 21
1 John 4:9-10
WRAP – Psalm 100:5
Numbers 23:19
Deuteronomy 31:8
Lamentations 3:22-23
Psalm 36:5
Hebrews 13:8

Chapter 7

Psalm 51:10-12
2 Corinthians 7:10
2 Samuel 11-12
Psalm 32, 38, 51
Psalm 38:6
Psalm 51:8
Psalm 38:10
Romans 8:13-14
1 John 1:8-9
Psalm 51:13

Philippians 4:8
1 Peter 1:22
Mark 12;30
John 16:22
Psalm 37:4
Leviticus 19:17
Matthew 6:21
Matthew 15:8
Matthew 15:18-20
Jeremiah 17:9-10
Hebrews 11:6
2 Peter 3:18
Romans 12:1-2
Colossians 3:2
Romans 8:5-6
WRAP – Ephesians 4:22-24

Chapter 10

1 John 3:1-3
Proverbs 3:5
Proverbs 3:6
John 15
Revelations 12:11
2 Timothy 1:7
2 Corinthians 10:3-5
John 17:17
Romans 12:1-3
Proverbs 4:23
Isaiah 26:3
Colossians 3:1-17
Philippians 4:6-9

Ephesians 4:20-24
2 Timothy 3:14-17
Psalm 139:17-18
WRAP - 2 Timothy 1:7

Chapter 11

Proverbs 16
Proverbs 16:16
Ephesians 4:1
Jeremiah 17:5-6
Jeremiah 17:9-10
Psalm 139:1-12, 23-24
Psalm 45:10
Galatians 1:10
James 5:9
1 Corinthians 15:33
2 Timothy 3:15-17
Colossians 3:9
Ephesians 4:22
Romans 13:12
Colossians 3:10
Colossians 3:12-14
Ephesians 4:24
Romans 13:14
Proverbs 6:23
1 John 5:3
1 John 2:5
Luke 9:23
WRAP – Colossians 3:9-10

Chapter 12

John 20:30-32
John 6:35
John 8:12
John 10:9
John 10:11
John 11:25
John 14:7
John 15:1-5
John 15:6-8
John 15:9
John 15:12-17
1 John 4:15-16
1 John 4:7-8
Psalm 16:11
Galatians 5:22
John 14:16
2 Peter 1:3-4
2 Peter 1:5-9
2 Peter 1:10
Psalm 1:3
WRAP – John 15:5

Chapter 13

2 Timothy 3:16-17
John 1:4-5
John 8:12
John 12:46
1 Peter 1:13-16
James 1:5-7
WRAP - 1 Peter 1:6-7
Ephesians 3:14-21

Resources by Chapter

All resources are available through the QR code. Scan the code for direct access to all WRAP Yourself in the Word resources or go to www.jonirosebrock.com or email:

joni@jonirosebrock.com.

Chapter 1

A sample WRAP journal page is available for download. Print as many copies as you need. Coming soon is a WRAP Yourself in the Word Journal.

Scripture writing plan www.ibelieve.com has past and current Scripture writing plans you can download. You can also go to Google or Pinterest and search for Scripture writing plans. You can also download the file that includes my first 90 days of writing Scripture. This document includes the first 90 verses from when I started writing Scripture daily.

Chapter 2

Self-Talk downloadable worksheet: Useful for personal exploration and comparing lies and truth in "what it" thinking to "even if' thinking. The worksheet is helpful in intentionally noticing the influences of thoughts and feelings on behaviors.

Growth Challenge: Write the following three verses: Philippians 4:8, 2 Corinthians 10:5b, Romans 12:1-2

Chapter 3

A list of my favorite online and printed Bible resources.

Growth Challenge: Memorize the books of the New Testament.

Chapter 4

Bonus chapter: DIG —Discover, Investigate, Grow, an inductive Bible study option. DIG into Psalm 1:1-3.

Growth Challenge: Read Psalm 119. Make two columns on your paper. As you read Psalm 119, list what you learn about God's Word, His attributes, or His power in the first column. Then, in the second column, list how you think or feel or what you are to do in response to His Word. This worksheet and other resources are located on the website.

Chapter 5

The prayer model is based on the Lord's Prayer. The worksheet and printable bookmark are available on the website.

Growth Challenge: WRAP each Scripture reference found in the chapter.

- Matthew 6:9-13
- Romans 8:26
- Psalm 18:6
- Psalm 34:17-18
- Psalm 139:23-24
- Psalm 3:11-12
- Hebrew 12:10-11
- Hebrew 4:12
- John 17:17
- 2 Timothy 3:16-17

Chapter 6

Growth Challenge: Schedule coffee or tea with a friend and share your faith stories. Be sure to include stories about your faith legacies and where you have found God to be faithful.

Chapter 7

Growth Challenge: Pray Psalm 139 back to God, pausing after each stanza, listening for God's response to you. Journal what you hear. Don't hear anything? Sit longer in silence, break the Psalm into shorter sections, and concentrate on one part each day. Do this daily for one week and notice the change in your thoughts. A helpful worksheet with the Psalm printed out, and other resources from this book are available.

Chapter 8

Growth Challenge: Consider how your daily life would change if you approached your circumstances and people from the perspective of victory as one who has overcome. Journal your thoughts, or better yet, have a deep, meaningful conversation about this perspective with a friend.

Chapter 9

Growth Challenge: Ask God to show you where your sinful nature controls your thoughts and feelings and where He would like you to allow the Spirit to control your mind. Listen, journal, and talk to a friend who can help you with accountability.

Chapter 10

Thought Inventory Journal – helpful in tracking your thoughts to notice patterns of emotions, thoughts, and repeated lies. A download is available on the website.

Growth Challenge: FAITH Map - Our faith is a gift through God's grace and where we begin all transformation and healing. Check out the FAITH Map on my website. Remember, you can easily access it using the QR code. You can use this tool in many ways: Bible Study, self-coaching, and evaluating where your Faith needs strengthening. Begin to consider: Where has God been faithful? What are your habits of abiding? How do you receive God's instruction?

How do you express thankfulness? Where do you place your hope for today or the future?

Chapter 11

Put off – Put on Reference Table – downloadable file.

Growth Challenge – Reread the chapter and ask God to help you listen to His Spirit with great attention. Journal your thoughts.

Chapter 12

Growth Challenge: Where do you find joy? Make a list. For three days, list ten joys in your life each day. If you find a lack of joy in your life, you should examine your habits of abiding.

Chapter 13

Growth Challenge: Pray Ephesians 3:14-21 for yourself.

Father, When I think of all you have provided, I fall to my knees and pray. You are Father, the Creator of everything in heaven and on earth. I pray from your glorious, unlimited resources that you will empower me with inner strength through the Spirit. I invite Christ to make his home in my heart as I trust in Him. Cause my roots to grow down into your love and keep me strong. God grant me the power to understand, as all God's people should, how wide, how long, how high, and how deep your love is. I want to experience the love of Christ, though it is too great to understand fully. I want to be made complete with all the fullness of life and power that comes from you. Now all glory to you, God, who is able, through your mighty power at work within us, to accomplish infinitely more than I might ask or think. Glory to you and Christ Jesus through all generations, forever and ever! Amen

Quotes by Chapter

Chapter 1 - Begin

But do not be afraid. The simple fact that you are more aware of your wounds shows that you have sufficient strength to face them. Your heart is greater than your wounds. Henri Nouwen

Chapter 2 - Write the Word

First, I do not sit down at my desk to put into verse something that is already clear in my mind. If it were clear in my mind, I should have no incentive or need to write about it. We do not write in order to be understood; we write in order to understand. C. S. Lewis

Chapter 3 - Read the Word

The word of God hidden in the heart is a stubborn voice to suppress. Billy Graham

Chapter 4 - Apply the Word

The essence of surrender is getting out of God's way so that He can do in us what He also wants to do through us. AW Tozer

Chapter 12 - Abide in the Vine

It is the Holy Spirit who encourages and enables us to abide. He teaches us the Word; He enables us to pray; He reveals our sins; He gives us the inward desire to obey God. Warren Wiersbe

Chapter 13 - Invitation to Grow in Godliness

All Scripture is inspired by God and is useful to teach us what is true and to make us realize what is wrong in our lives. It corrects us when we are wrong and teaches us to do what is right. God uses it to prepare and equip his people to do every good work.
2 Timothy 3:16-17

www.ingramcontent.com/pod-product-compliance
Lightning Source LLC
Chambersburg PA
CBHW021715120626
46545CB00004B/1577